The Greatest Love Movies

More Than Just a Kiss

THE GREATEST LOVE MOVIES

WHITE STAR PUBLISHERS

PROJECT EDITOR   VALERIA MANFERTO DE FABIANIS

GRAPHIC DESIGN   CLARA ZANOTTI

EDITORIAL COORDINATION   LAURA ACCOMAZZO

WS White Star Publishers® is a registered
trademark property of Edizioni White Star s.r.l.

© 2010, 2011 Edizioni White Star s.r.l.
Via M. Germano, 10
13100 Vercelli, Italy
www.whitestar.it

ISBN 978-88-544-0610-0 \
1 2 3 4 5 6   15 14 13 12 11

Printed in China

TEXT BY
ROBERT MARICH

CONTENTS

Introduction   Page 10

1931	CITY LIGHTS (Charlie Chaplin)	P.18
1934	IT HAPPENED ONE NIGHT (Frank Capra)	P.24
1935	ANNA KARENINA (Clarence Brown)	P.30
1939	GONE WITH THE WIND (Victor Fleming)	P.38
1939	NINOTCHKA (Ernst Lubitsch)	P.48
1942	CASABLANCA (Michael Curtiz)	P.50
1950	CINDERELLA (Clyde Geronimi / Wilfred Jackson / Hamilton Luske)	P.56
1951	THE AFRICAN QUEEN (John Huston)	P.66
1952	THE QUIET MAN (John Ford)	P.72
1953	ROMAN HOLIDAY (William Wyler)	P.80
1954	SABRINA (Billy Wilder)	P.86
1955	LADY AND THE TRAMP (Clyde Geronimi / Wilfred Jackson / Hamilton Luske)	P.94
1955	LOVE IS A MANY-SPLENDORED THING (Henry King)	P.98
1956	HIGH SOCIETY (Charles Walters)	P.100
1956	BUS STOP (Joshua Logan)	P.106
1957	AN AFFAIR TO REMEMBER (Leo McCarey)	P.108
1959	SLEEPING BEAUTY (Clyde Geronimi / Les Clark / Eric Larson / Wolfgang Reitherman)	P.110
1963	YESTERDAY, TODAY AND TOMORROW (Vittorio De Sica)	P.118
1964	MY FAIR LADY (George Cukor)	P.124
1965	DOCTOR ZHIVAGO (David Lean)	P.130
1966	A MAN AND A WOMAN (Claude Lelouch)	P.134
1967	BAREFOOT IN THE PARK (Gene Saks)	P.136
1967	BONNIE AND CLYDE (Arthur Penn)	P.140
1968	ROMEO AND JULIET (Franco Zeffirelli)	P.142
1970	LOVE STORY (Arthur Hiller)	P.146
1973	THE WAY WE WERE (Sydney Pollack)	P.150
1977	ANNIE HALL (Woody Allen)	P.152

Index page 284   -   Photo Credits page 286

P.156	ON GOLDEN POND (Mark Rydell)	1981
P.160	AN OFFICER AND A GENTLEMAN (Taylor Hackford)	1982
P.162	OUT OF AFRICA (Sydney Pollack)	1985
P.170	A ROOM WITH A VIEW (James Ivory)	1985
P.174	LADYHAWKE (Richard Donner)	1985
P.178	MOONSTRUCK (Norman Jewison)	1987
P.180	WHEN HARRY MET SALLY... (Rob Reiner)	1989
P.184	GHOST (Jerry Zucker)	1990
P.188	PRETTY WOMAN (Garry Marshall)	1990
P.194	BEAUTY AND THE BEAST (Gary Trousdale / Kirk Wise)	1991
P.198	ALADDIN (Ron Clements / John Musker)	1992
P.202	SLEEPLESS IN SEATTLE (Nora Ephron)	1993
P.206	LEGENDS OF THE FALL (Edward Zwick)	1994
P.212	POCAHONTAS (Mike Gabriel / Eric Goldberg)	1995
P.216	THE BRIDGES OF MADISON COUNTY (Clint Eastwood)	1995
P.218	THE ENGLISH PATIENT (Anthony Minghella)	1996
P.222	TITANIC (James Cameron)	1997
P.228	SHAKESPEARE IN LOVE (John Madden)	1998
P.234	SHREK (Andrew Adamson / Vicky Jenson)	2001
P.240	MY BIG FAT GREEK WEDDING (Joel Zwick)	2002
P.244	SOMETHING'S GOTTA GIVE (Nancy Meyers)	2003
P.250	50 FIRST DATES (Peter Segal)	2004
P.252	A VERY LONG ENGAGEMENT (Jean-Pierre Jeunet)	2004
P.258	KING KONG (Peter Jackson)	2005
P.264	MAMMA MIA! (Phyllida Lloyd)	2008
P.270	TWILIGHT (Catherine Hardwicke)	2008
P.274	COCO BEFORE CHANEL (Anne Fontaine)	2009
P.280	AVATAR (James Cameron)	2009

P. 8 - 9   Katharine Hepburn and Spencer Tracy in "Woman of the Year", 1942.

« I shall stop loving you when I have finished counting the stars. »

JULIET CAPULET (Romeo and Juliet)

The way movies view love can best be summed up as the following: love is a comedy. More often than not, it is absurd, silly and/or ridiculous in what makes audiences laugh out loud. Sometimes, the comedy is downright farcical. In other instances, it is warm and amusing, which elicits restrained chuckles from the audience.

But the common denominator is that love is usually played for laughs on the silver screen. Well over half the films in this book are romantic comedies because that's what Hollywood and Europe churn out year after year.

In an example of that chuckle humor, Billy Crystal perceptively points out the quirks of the Meg Ryan character that he finds so endearing, after years of being just platonic friends in "When Harry Met Sally...".

"I love that you get a little crinkle above your nose when you're looking at me like I'm nuts," an excited Crystal tells Ryan as their relationship transitions from friendship to romance. "I love that you are the last person I want to talk to before I go to sleep at night and it's not because I'm lonely... I came here tonight because when you realize you want to spend the rest of your life with somebody, you want the rest of your life to start as soon as possible."

The humor can be delivered by the most unlikely characters as well. In "Beauty and the Beast," an "enchanted" Clock that has human-like characteristics coaches The Beast on how to charm the pretty peasant girl Belle, in a bit of laugh-out-loud humor. "Well," says the animated time-piece Clock, "there are the usual things: flowers, chocolates and promises you don't intend to keep."

What's that? Not keeping promises when romancing? Shocking!

Of course, the remainder of love movies in this book play it straight by making romance into serious drama. In "Twilight," the character portrayed by Robert Pattinson tells Kristen Stewart that he's no good for her, but "I don't have the strength to stay away from you anymore." Stewart replies in a low, quiet voice, "Then don't."

That is about a sexy as it gets with all your clothes on, and this scene has teenage girls around the world swooning!

For sophisticated audiences, there is the romantic tragedy of "The Bridges of Madison County," when Clint Eastwood's character says in a halting voice,

"It seems right now all that I've ever done in my life has been making my way here to you. If I have to think about leaving here tomorrow without you I..." He doesn't finish the sentence as he hugs and kisses Meryl Streep. "Oh my god," she finally says in tears. "What are we going to do?"

It's scenes like these that shape the world's view of romance because movies drive popular culture more than sociologists, teachers and even clergy.

"Bridges of Madison County," "Twilight," "Beauty and the Beast" and "When Harry Met Sally..." are among the 55 movies profiled in this book. The films date back from the talkie movie era (there's one silent film, Charlie Chaplin's memorable "City Lights"). The stars in this book include Humphrey Bogart, Greta Garbo, Omar Sharif, Sophia Loren, Meg Ryan, Julia Roberts, Tom Hanks and Audrey Tautou. The directors include Billy Wilder, Claude Lelouch, Sydney Pollack, Franco Zeffirelli, Clint Eastwood and James Cameron.

Why did we pick these particular films?

They are all films that we feel have enduring popularity with audiences, with some having an added bonus of being truly important milestones in cinema history. The stars, stories, location backdrops and history are of interest to movie aficionados. In the book, the movies are presented in chronological based on year of theatrical release.

And the movies in this book aren't all from Hollywood because half a dozen European films are included. The films aren't all live-action either because some romantic animated films tell simple but poignant love stories. Nobody can watch the majestic ballroom dancing scene in Disney's "Beauty and the Beast" without a heart-felt sigh over the grandeur on the screen and the tragedy of the story.

So these films aren't just box-office hits in the romance genre, although there are plenty of those too. "Gone With the Wind," "My Fair Lady," "Titanic" and "Avatar" are leading films in box office that serve up plenty of romance.

The 55 profiles of individual movies in this book provide interesting background not visible on the screen such as career achievements of talent involved, context in cinema history and interesting anecdotes. Further the write-ups of individual movies take pains to describe the films without giving away plot twists in films (commonly referred to as "spoilers") that would ruined the surprise for first-time viewers. For example, "The English Patient" spins an intricate web of mystery, but the book the doesn't reveal key plot twists that would spoil the surprise.

Of course, for some well-known films, there's no need to conceal plot turns because they are so well known. Zefirelli's "Romeo and Juliet" uses the dialog from the actual Shakespearean play, so the tragedy at the end comes as no surprise. After all, the play's the famous closing line of narration has been repeated to countless audiences and in literature classrooms for centuries: "For never was a story of more woe than this of Juliet and her Romeo."

The films in this book provide a roadmap to film history. "It Happened One Night" from 1934 (second oldest film in the book) presents Clark Gable and Claudette Colbert sharing a motel room separated only by a blanket hanging across their room. So how did director Frank Capra get away with two unmarried people sleeping in the same room given Hollywood studios' code for on-screen morality? The answer: The studios began enforcing rules that would forbid such scenes just after "It Happened One Night" was made so it is one of the last films not caught up in the formal restrictions.

For decades thereafter, Hollywood filmmakers were amazingly clever in conveying romance without nudity, steamy passion in love making, coarse language and overtly suggestive situations. Films could never even imply sex occurred off-screen between couples not married to each other. And even married couples were shown to sleep in separate beds—what became known as "Hollywood twin beds." Films like "Casablanca," "Roman Holiday," "Sabrina," "Bus Stop" and "An Affair to Remember" enthralled audiences despite the constraints of this so-called Production Code voluntarily enforced by the studios to avoid government censorship and placate moral crusaders.

The code was swept away gradually from 1959-68 under pressure from changing society and filmmakers. "Doctor Zhivago" and "Barefoot in the Park" are Hollywood studio films in this transitional period.

By the 1970s, the New Hollywood movement championing realism swept the U.S. film industry, which allowed studios to distribute such raw and anti-social films as "Bonnie and Clyde" and off-color social satire in "Annie Hall." The realism didn't have to be jarring but simply less idolized. There's an unblinking view of life and love in "Out of Africa," "Legends of the Fall" and "Pretty Woman."

in "Out of Africa," "Meryl Streep is unfaithful to her unfaithful husband, Julia Ormond ends up marrying the least appealing of her suitors in "Legends of the Fall," and Julia Roberts has a checkered past in "Pretty Woman." They are closer to the true-life that audiences live than the sanitized culture enforced by studios in the on-screen morality code.

European films didn't have a similar constraints. Sophia Loren is a happy hooker of "Yesterday, Today and Tomorrow," formal society's rigidness gets skewered by "A Room with a View" and Audrey Tautou refuses to accept the official story of her love's wartime death in "A Very Long Engagement."

There were some good things about the constraints of the studio system in years gone by. Studio bosses wielded editing snippers that cut film running times to a crisp length of 90-100 minutes in most cases. In recent years, filmmakers have routinely pushed running times to a bloated 150 minutes and more for even simple stories. An epic running length does not ensure an epic movie.

A common lament by film fans about movies today is that "They don't make them like they used to!" – which refers to earnest romantic stories and larger-than-life stars. But it's not possible to make commercial cinema films in the same way as Hollywood's golden era because of the influence of TV.

The modern film industry is competing against every movie ever made that is available on TV, DVD and video-on-demand. And TV series serve up lots of conventional romance comedy to an extent that audiences are saturated with this genre.

So movies need to present new thrills, twists and a contemporary context. So we have anti-heroes as well as heroes. Some serve up dubious morality, which is a far cry from the clear-cut good/bad of Hollywood's golden era. In "Legends of the Fall," Brad Pitt is the most appealing male lead, yet his character is self indulgent, aloof and self destructive in the mold of the New Hollywood anti-hero.

And stars today aren't put on pedestals and protected as was the case when the studio system controlled talent that was under exclusive contract. These days, stars get divorced—sometimes frequently—and their various foibles are covered in great detail by a scandal-loving press. This makes them rather ordinary instead of titans living in the transcendental world that Hollywood was able to create decades ago.

Writing a book is an individual endeavor and so here are some personal observations and reactions of your author:

In researching "City Lights" (the oldest movie in this book), I was surprised to come across a contemporary review in "Variety" of this Chaplin romantic comedy that was written by the grandfather of my wife! "Perhaps the high spot is a burlesque prize fight which in rehearsal time alone must have taken weeks to shoot," wrote Sid Silverman in his 1931 review.

My father took me to see "Doctor Zhivago" in its theatrical release when I was a young lad in Chicago and I remember being impressed with the screen images but perplexed by Russian history. Seeing it again reminds me how my father, a refugee from post WWII Eastern Europe, viewed novelist Boris Pasternak's savage critique of the social upheaval with a personal perspective that is the backdrop to the romance between Omar Sharif and Julie Christie.

If you like dogs (like me), then you'll love "Lady and the Tramp" for its many small but brilliant insights on canines. Through most of the movie, humans are shown from the waist down to give "dog's eye view" of world and Tramp's exuberant character captures the spirit of happily yapping dogs everywhere.

I try to imagine what the alternative reality films would have traveled if the studios had not enforced the morality code in 1934 and "It Happened One Night" would have been the launch rather than conclusion of realistic screen portrayals. Films turned out okay with the morality code, but they would have been quite a bit different without.

"On Golden Pond" is an extraordinary achievement by making a drama about two old people and their dysfunctional family a box office hit. Usually, the best such films can hope for is critical acclaim and only most commercial success.

Marilyn Monroe displays an amazingly diverse range of talent in the off-beat Western comedy "Bus Stop," including singing off key on purpose to portray an untalented young saloon singer. Surely, she would have eventually won an Oscar that eluded her if she had aged and segued into purely dramatic role. But she died of from an overdose of prescription drugs at age 36.

There are so many memorable scenes in the 55 films that it's hard to pick one or even a few as favorites. But one famous scene in "My Big Fat Greek Wedding" is ideal for an ending on this occasion.

Nia Vardalos portrays a woman on her wedding night who gets very last-minute and unwelcome instructions from her mother portrayed by Lainie Kazan (the film's star Vardalos wrote the screenplay).

Trying to be helpful, mom played by Kazan, says, "I want to talk to you. This is a very special night for you. You have your duties....On my wedding night, my mother, she said to me, 'Greek women, we may be lambs in the kitchen, but we are tigers in the bedroom.'"

A wide-eyed and mortified Vardalos replies nearly frozen in shock:

"Euw. Please let that be the end of your speech."

This book celebrates these films.

MORE THAN
JUST A KISS

« I want more...
I want
the fairy tale.»

VIVIAN WARD (Julia Roberts) "Pretty Woman"

When "City Lights" was released in 1931, the "talking film" era was already three years old and audiences pretty much ignored "silent" films. But its star, writer and director Charlie Chaplin was such a box office draw that he was able to make this black-and-white romantic comedy as a silent film, though with synchronized music and sound effects from the new audio technology.

Despite being a throwback, "City Lights" proved to be a hit with audiences. The 1 hour, 23 minute film, that was first distributed by United Artists was then, and still is today, hailed as a masterpiece by film critics.

The plot revolves around Chaplin's shabby Little Tramp character raising money so a pretty young woman who is blind can afford an operation that will give her eyesight. He meets the blind woman on the street where she sells flowers to passersby, and Chaplin obviously becomes smitten with her.

Because Chaplin does manage to scrape together money, he seems to be a man of wealth since the blind woman can't see his tattered clothes. When the blind woman's grandmother marvels later that the benefactor she's never met must be rich, the blind woman replies with a far-off and dreamy look on her face, "Yes, but he's more than that." Because this is a silent film, dialog is projected on screen as written words on what is called an intertitle—which is also called a title card.

As "City Lights" progresses, Chaplin has misadventures with a drunken rich man, the city sanitation department, prize-fighters and the police. These are vintage Chaplin plot turns, in that the Little Tramp always tries to do good, but an indifferent world thwarts him at every turn. Ordinary situations inadvertently go awry, with the result being situational and slapstick comedy that centers on the physically-elastic and innocent Chaplin.

One of the film's famous lines resonated with audiences battered by the Great Depression of the 1930s with its message not to be sorrowful with today's woes. "Tomorrow the birds will sing," Chaplin tells a depressed soul. "Be brave. Face life!"

THE LITTLE TRAMP CHARACTER PLAYED BY CHARLIE CHAPLIN COOKS UP MONEY-MAKING SCHEMES AFTER LEARNING A COSTLY SURGICAL PROCEDURE CAN RESTORE SIGHT TO A BLIND YOUNG WOMAN (IN WINDOW CENTER TOP) WHO IS OBJECT OF HIS AFFECTIONS.

1931
City Lights

Directed by CHARLIE CHAPLIN

Starring: CHARLIE CHAPLIN (The little tramp) VIRGINIA CHERRILL (Blind Girl)
HARRY MYERS / HANK MANN

Music by CHARLIE CHAPLIN

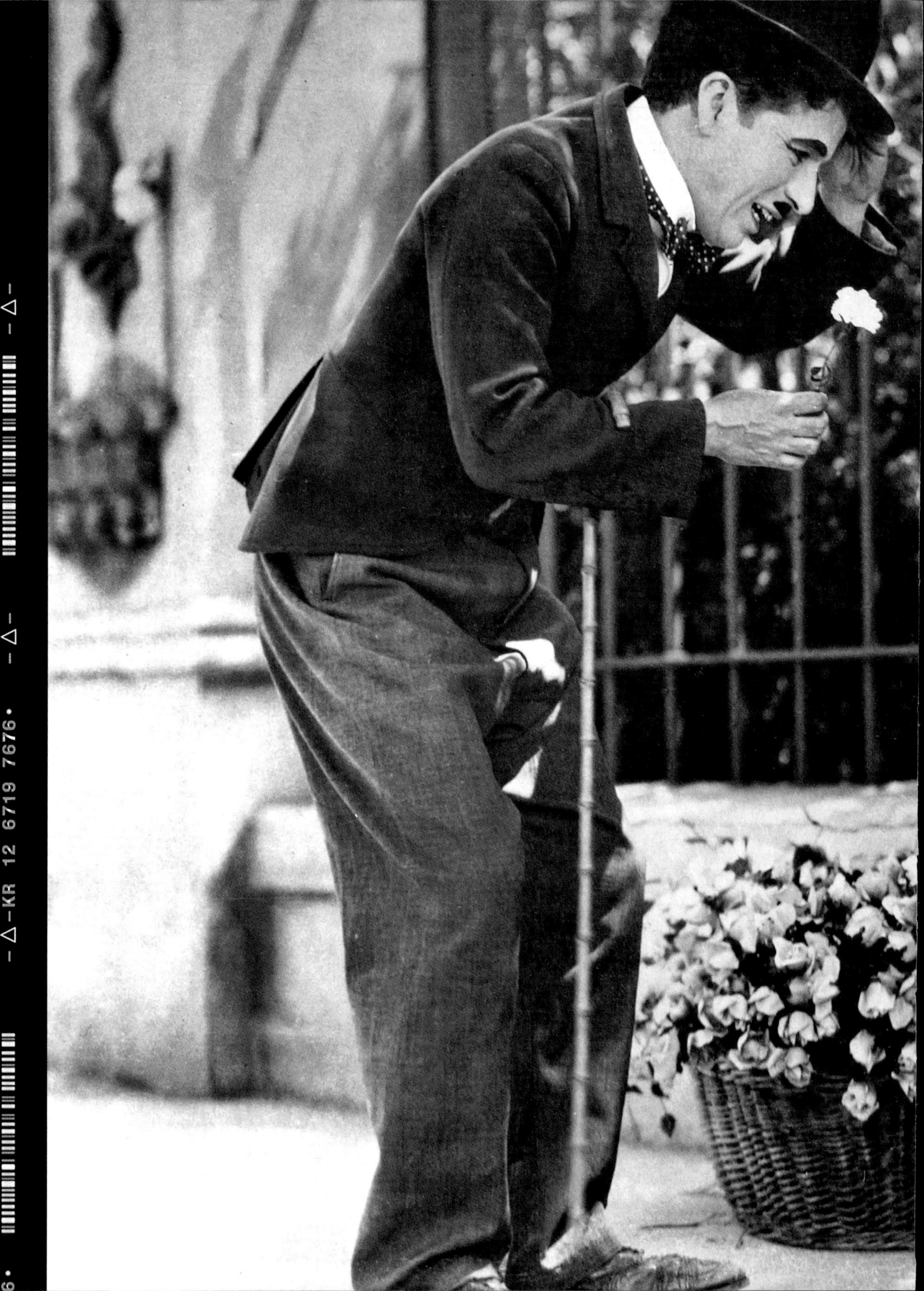
-Δ-KR 12 6719 7676•

A blind young woman selling flowers on the street in the Depression Era 1930s thinks the man who is buying flowers is wealthy, like her other customers. But he's really the penniless but good-hearted Little Tramp character played by Charlie Chaplin.

«-Charlie Chaplin:
...I wanted the music to be a counterpoint of grace and charm, to express sentiment, without which, as Hazlitt says, a work of art is incomplete.-»

The final scene is hailed as one of cinema's greatest. The pretty flower woman who by then can see (courtesy of medical treatment made possible by Chaplin funds) realizes through a touch of his hand and arm that the Little Tramp standing before her is her savior. The scene is long on sentimentality and short on a dialog as intertitle card has the shocked woman simply saying, "You?"

"City Lights" makes sparse use of dialog intertitles. Instead, the movie relies on Chaplin's genius for comic pantomime that helps convey conversation and situations to the audience.

Chaplin's Little Tramp is the most famous character in movies from the early 20th Century, captivating audiences around the world since 1914. The signature look is Chaplin twirling a cane as he walks in a waddling manner while wearing a derby hat (which he incessantly raises with a tip of the hand in a nervous tick to be polite), baggy pants, tight suit-coat, oversized shoes and small mustache (a big mustache would hide facial expression).

Another constant is that the Little Tramp is always looking for love. His pursuit of romance provides amusing story elements that are often slightly sad—which plumb the emotions of the audience. The Little Tramp is also a realization of the old proverb that the outer shell doesn't reveal the inner truth, because his character is good-hearted and dignified despite a shabby appearance.

In 2008, the American Film Institute listed "City Lights" first among the Top 10 Romantic Comedies up to that time. This created a minor sensation because the silent film ranked higher than nine other talkies including "Annie Hall," "It Happened One Night" and "Roman Holiday."

Expectations were low when "It Happened One Night" reached theaters in 1934, including by those who worked on the film. But the romantic comedy starring Clark Gable and Claudette Colbert became a surprise hit with audiences. Then, it made Oscar history by being the first film to sweep the top five major categories including Best Picture—a feat not again duplicated for another four decades.

Colbert portrays a helpless heiress on the run from her wealthy family and Gable is a street-wise newspaper reporter who by accident becomes her travelling companion.

In a famous scene as they try to hitch a ride with passing cars, Colbert lifts her dress by the roadside as if adjusting her stockings, exposing her sexy leg. The first automobile to pass immediately stops to give Colbert and Gable a lift, leaving Gable irritated by his own earlier failure to get them a ride using the standard outstretched "thumb" hand signal.

"Why didn't you take off all your clothes?" snaps Gable, annoyed that Colbert bettered him by using her feminine wiles. "You could have stopped 40 cars."

Brimming with satisfaction, Colbert teases, "Well, ooh, I'll remember that when we need 40 cars."

"It Happened One Night" is filled with clever dialog like that, and also 1930s period slang like "being a sucker" for a fool, calling regular-guy men "mugs," and a pretty woman "a dame." The movie takes place over several days—not in "one night" as the title suggests.

As the 1 hour, 45 minute movie unfolds, Gable realizes that his new-found travelling companion is a rich woman who is the object of a nationwide hunt and big cash reward. And, of course, there are also romantic complications as the two opposite personalities become attracted to each other.

"Would you believe it?" Colbert tells Gable over breakfast, marveling at the turn of events in her up-to-now sheltered life. "This is the first time I've ever been alone with a man!" A not-impressed Gable simply grunts, "Yeah?"

Colbert continues "It's a wonder I'm not panic-stricken." Not believing she's such an ingénue, Gable answers, "You're doing all right."

The black-and-white film is historic as the first complete sweep of the main Oscars—Best Picture, Best Actor for Gable, Best Actress for Colbert, Best Adapted Screenplay and Best Director for Frank Capra—coming in the seventh year of the Academy Awards. "It Happened One Night" won in every category it was nominated. The film was distributed by minor studio Columbia Pictures, which rented Gable's acting services from giant Metro-Goldwyn-Mayer where Gable was under contract but idle at the time.

1934

It Happened One Night

Directed by FRANK CAPRA

Starring: CLARK GABLE (Peter Warne) CLAUDETTE COLBERT (Ellie Andrews)
WALTER CONNOLLY / ROSCOE KARNS / ALAN HALE

Music by LOUIS SILVERS

CLARK GABLE CARRIES CLAUDETTE COLBERT ACROSS A WOODED AREA AS THEY AVOID PUBLIC PLACES TO EVADE DETECTIVES SENT BY HER WEALTHY FATHER. THOUGH THEY HAVE TO SLEEP OUTDOORS WHILE HIDING OUT, NEITHER SEEMS TO MIND TOO MUCH.

On the run with little money, streetwise Clark Gable instructs Claudette Colbert in how to hitch a ride with thumb ups in hopes a passing automobile driver will stop to give them a lift.

Claudette Colbert slowly warms to the always-resourceful Clark Gable, who has no trouble sleeping in a sitting position on a long ride, shortly after they battle for scarce seats on a crowded long-haul passenger bus.

Capra, who is known for his portrayals of ordinary people as extraordinary, and for his films affirming American ideals, is a giant of Hollywood with three Oscar wins and three additional nominations as a director. Among his many other well-known films are "It's A Wonderful Life" and "Mr. Smith Goes to Washington," both starring Jimmy Stewart.

Just after "It Happened One Night" was made, Hollywood's major studios began enforcing an industry code requiring strict morality in movies, and that code would have meant drastic changes for this film. Most conspicuously, it would have forbidden a signature scene showing Gable and Colbert forced by a rainstorm to share opposite sides of a motel room separated only by a blanket hanging along a rope for privacy. The reason: they are not married and, in fact, there's a question if Colbert is legally married to another man.

"I just had the unpleasant sensation of hearing you referred to as my husband," a peeved Colbert tells Gable after walking through the courtyard of the motel. "Oh yah. I forgot to tell you about that," replies a nonchalant Gable in their room. "I registered as Mister and Missus... (But) if you're nursing any silly notion that I'm interested in you, forget it."

"It Happened One Night" is of historical significance beyond its amazing Oscar haul, because it presented a more daring view of romance and permissible situations than studios would later allow.

◄ Forced to share opposite ends of a motel room because of a rain storm, Claudette Colbert and Clark Gable are separated by a hanging blanket, in a then-daring story situation for 1934 Hollywood cinema because they are not married to each other.

Movies based on Leo Tolstoy's novel "Anna Karenina" span a century back to the silent film era, and the most famous is the 1935 rendition from Metro-Goldwyn-Mayer starring Greta Garbo.

Audiences need to have a handkerchief at the ready. "Anna Karenina" is a romantic tragedy of passion and loss that lacks a happy Hollywood ending. The beautiful and aloof Garbo stars as a high society wife trapped in an unhappy marriage to a government official in this opulent period drama set in 1870s Czarist Russia. The black-and-white talkie is a remake of a silent film that also starred Garbo.

Garbo—whose character's name is the movie's title—is a married mother who is wooed by a dashing and single military officer, played by Fredric March. As they play croquet at an outdoor party, March asks Garbo if she thinks they are being watched and the object of gossip. "Watched?" Garbo replies dryly, looking away at the other guests. "We've being devoured."

With a debonair quality accented by a stylish thin, wide mustache, March plays Count Vronsky, who is a lady's man and plays the part by living in high style.

The film is not heavy with passionate kisses or embraces, but rather the romance plays out through intrigue in a dense web drawn from the complex Tolstoy novel. Russia's aristocracy is shown as superficial and its men are shallow adventurers. But the movie boils this story down to a streamlined 1 hour, 35 minutes on the cinema screen.

The aristocracy's emphasis on society position over matters of the heart is brought into sharp focus by Garbo's cold husband, played by Basil Rathbone. "I am not speaking as a jealous husband," he tells Garbo while pacing across their bedroom, "but as a man of the world who knows there are certain rules of decorum that can't be disregarded with impunity." Rathbone continues, "I'm not inquiring into your feelings, Anna. I have no right to ferret into your soul. I am concerned only with appearances."

DRESSED IN OPULENT HIGH FASHION OF 1870S RUSSIA, GRETA GARBO IS LEFT TO WRESTLE WITH HER PERSONAL DEMONS AND PONDER ON-AND-OFF REGRETS ABOUT HER DECISION TO CHOOSE REAL LOVE OVER HER UNHAPPY MARRIAGE.

1935
Anna Karenina

Directed by CLARENCE BROWN

Starring: GRETA GARBO (Anna Karenina)   FREDRIC MARCH (Count Vronsky)
FREDDIE BARTHOLOMEW / MAUREEN O'SULLIVAN / MAY ROBSON

Music by HERBERT STOTHART

Greta Garbo comforts her sick son in a surprise visit long after she leaves her husband for the love of another man. Despite her husband banishing her from her former home, the household servants disregard standing orders not to let her in, because she had been kind to them.

Garbo struggles with her two lives as respectable high society wife while also seeing March on the side. March eventually finds this unacceptable, delivering this ultimatum. "I'm weighing my words very carefully," he says, holding Garbo's arms. "For you, if need be, I'm willing to give up everything. Will you do as much for me?"

Garbo struggles to respond but admits she can't because that would separate her from the young son who adores her. Eventually Garbo does break away from her unhappy marriage to be with March, but she suffers the consequences by becoming a societal outcast.

The backdrop to this woeful tale of love are lavish balls in grand halls with orchestras playing, and private parties at long dinner tables—all under glittering chandeliers and with servants everywhere. The costumes, setting and photography project an over-the-top decadence that foreshadows the fall of the Russian aristocracy.

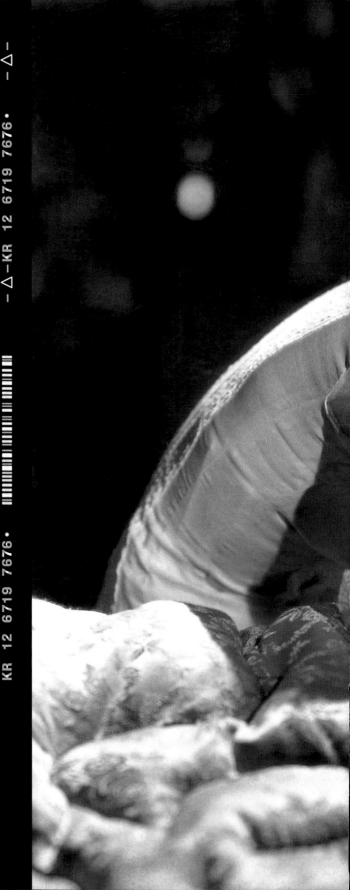

The 1935 film received no Oscar nominations, even though the performances are top notch and the opulent settings and costuming are breathtaking. Yet the actors—mostly European—and talent behind the camera—led by Americas—are still distinguished.

In her full career, silver screen superstar Garbo would be nominated three times for Oscars as an actress and receive a career achievement award. Leading man March would win two Oscars in his career and be nominated three other times. In later years, Garbo's screen husband Rathbone would go on to star as detective Sherlock Holmes in a memorable series of B movies and also receive two Oscar nominations. Maureen O'Sullivan—who portrays a young woman battered by romantic intrigue—is a Hollywood legend and the mother of actress Mia Farrow.

Behind the camera, American director Clarence Brown received nominations for five Oscars in his full career. "Anna Karenina" was produced by legendary Hollywood producer David O. Selznick, whose many producing credits include "Gone with the Wind."

« - ... I'M WILLING TO GIVE UP EVERYTHING -»

Greta Grabo finds romantic bliss when she hooks up with dashing military officer Fredric March, but they are ostracized by proper Russian Czarist society because she abandons her marriage to be with March.

1. Greta Garbo travels in a passenger train compartment across a frozen Russian winter landscape. Nineteenth Century Russia is a grand backdrop for the turbulent life and loves of the upper-class character portrayed by Garbo.

2. Greta Garbo was a top 1930s Hollywood star whose beauty and acting skill captivated audiences around the world. In addition to popularity with audiences, the Swedish-born actress received artistic recognition with three Oscar nominations for performances and a career achievement award.

Hollywood's greatest year is said to be 1939, which is when "Gone with the Wind" won the Oscar for Best Picture. The epic romance beat these time-honored movies: "The Wizard of Oz," "Stagecoach," "Wuthering Heights" and "Ninotchka."

"Gone with the Wind," which runs an epic 3 hours, 58 minutes, presents the tumultuous life and many loves of vivacious Southern belle Scarlett O'Hara, portrayed by Vivien Leigh—around the U.S. Civil War of the early 1860s. At first, Leigh seems little more than a strong-willed social schemer bent on exploiting her exquisite good looks and endlessly flirting with men. But she shrewdly navigates the poverty after war, becoming a successful businesswoman and savior for her family, though she remains a shallow schemer in regards to romance.

When she accepts a marriage proposal from Clark Gable, she admits, "If I said that I was madly in love with you, you'd know that I was lying. But you've always said we have a lot in common."

Gable interrupts, "Yes, you are right, my dear. I'm not any more in love with you than you with me...Well, what kind of (wedding) ring would you like, my darling?"

Gable portrays a likeable rogue who, like Leigh, comes from Southern wealth. He becomes independently super-rich in the Civil War by smuggling goods around the North's shipping blockade of the South.

After his turbulent marriage to Leigh sours, she wails, 'what will become of me?' to which Gable delivers perhaps the most famous line in the history of cinema. "Frankly, my dear, I don't give a damn," he says matter-of-factly as he heads into the foggy night. Only then does Leigh realize how much she really loves Gable.

1939

Gone With the Wind

Directed by VICTOR FLEMING

Starring: VIVIEN LEIGH (Scarlett O'Hara) CLARK GABLE (Rhett Butler)
LESLIE HOWARD / OLIVIA DE HAVILLAND / HATTIE MCDANIEL

Music by MAX STEINER

CLARK GABLE AND VIVIEN LEIGH EMBRACE AFTER YEARS OF A HANDS-OFF, LOVE-HATE RELATIONSHIP THAT MORPHS INTO MARRIAGE. THEY ARE BOTH STRONG-WILLED, SOCIALLY SKILLED, SURVIVORS AMID HARD TIMES AND THEY ARE SOMETIMES UNPRINCIPLED—IN OTHER WORDS PERFECT FOR EACH OTHER.

Gable received an Oscar nomination for his performance, which is among 13 for "Gone with the Wind." The film won in eight categories (plus one technical and one honorary award—some count 10 wins with these). That huge victory haul is doubly impressive given stiff competition from the class of 1939 and also because many of those wins came in major categories. In addition to Best Picture, its Academy Award victories include Leigh as Best Lead Actress, Victor Fleming as Best Director, Hattie McDaniel as Best Supporting Actress, Best Color Cinematography and Best Screenplay.

While acclaimed artistically, "Gone with the Wind" serves up plenty of melodrama as Leigh has designs on a noble character portrayed by Leslie Howard, who is married. When Howard introduces Leigh to his fiancée, Leigh responds with a sly maliciousness, "You must'n flatter me, Melanie, and say things you don't mean."

Howard's wife Melanie is portrayed by Olivia de Havilland, who is a saintly and eventually becomes genuine friends with Leigh. De Havilland received an Oscar nomination for Best Supporting Actress.

1. Vivien Leigh will suffer the pain of a tight corset to make her waist-line thinner. Her plantation servant—the sassy and shrewd Mammy portrayed by Hattie McDaniel—applies the squeeze. McDaniel won an Oscar for Best Supporting Actress.

2. Clark Gable comes from money and a good family in 1860s southern America, but he's got a wild streak and isn't afraid to push the limits of proper behavior. For the turbulence and poverty of the Civil War, those traits are useful for survival.

▲ 1

1. and 2. Vivien Leigh's husband dies in the Civil War, so she dons a black dress of a mourning widow of 1860s Southern high society. But she's cheered by her dance partner, the loveable rogue Clark Gable, at a festive social event.

«-Rhett Butler

You're looking pale. Is there a shortage of rouge?
Or can this wonders mean you've been missing me?-»

Vivien Leigh and Clark Gable seem to be made for each other as ▶
survivors when their society breaks down—both can be ruthless
when necessary and yet also high-minded at times. Yet, their
own weaknesses tear them apart.

«-Scarlett O'Hara:
As God is my witness, as God is my witness, they're not going
to lick me! I'm going to live through this, and when it's all over,
I'll never be hungry again - no, nor any of my folks!
If I have to lie, steal, cheat, or kill, as God is my witness,
I'll never be hungry again."-»

The film, which was a blockbuster in theaters for Metro-Goldwyn-Mayer, is based on a best-selling novel published three years earlier, the title of which references that South's way of life is swept away by the Civil War. The characters live in opulence before the war, and poverty and humiliation immediately afterwards.

Many white Southerners see the movie as a touchstone celebrating a chivalrous and admirable society that was lost, and the film is full of disparagement of "Yankees"—or victorious Northerners from the Civil War. But others are not so sentimental, because human slavery was integral to growing cotton at the large plantation farms.

The movie's dialog is peppered with bits of regional Southern vernacular: "great balls of fire" and "great jehosophat" as exclamations; "darkies" for black people and "it just aint fittn'" for poor manners.

Like films of that era, "Gone with the Wind" is crafted to be suitable for a general audience, although viewers will see some marital bedroom quarreling, females in physical jeopardy, deaths including one child and bloody hospital/battlefield scenes during wartime.

McDaniel, who portrayed Leigh's brassy and wise servant Mammy, is the first black person to win an Oscar in acting. In one memorable exchange, she warns Leigh with this pearl of wisdom laced with dialect grammar, "What's gentlemen says and what they thinks are two different things." The Mammy and Scarlett characters represent the indomitable spirit of the South.

«-Scarlett O'Hara:
Oh, Rhett!... Rhett,
if you go, where shall I go?
What shall I do?

-Rhett Butler:
Frankly, my dear,
I don't give a damn!»

Vivien Leigh is a quintessential Southern belle
from America's Civil War era of the early 1860s.
She pretty, socially active, manipulative, able to
shift from warm to cold-blooded in an instant, and
determined to get what she wants.

Greta Garbo was one of the few stars of the silent-movie era to successfully transition to "talkies" because audiences remained enchanted by her gaze, which could range from soft warmth to radiant luminosity. In "Ninotchka," Garbo portrays hard-as-nails Russian apparatchik (a Communist party worker) Ninotchka, who sent to Paris on Soviet business and who warms to capitalism's bourgeoisie charms as well to her co-star Melvyn Douglas.

Though Garbo is top billed, Douglas gets the juicier role, allowing for more nuances. He portrays a sly antagonist in legal battle over control of Russian jewels in France, besides being Garbo's romantic interest.

"Love is a romantic designation for a most ordinary biological, or shall we say, chemical process," a rigidly-Bolshevik Garbo tells Douglas. "A lot of nonsense is talked and written about it." Responds a wide-eyed and romance-eager Douglas, "What can I possibly do to encourage such an impulse in you?...Ninotchka, it's midnight. One half of Paris is making love to the other half."

As the movie unfolds, Garbo warms to the West and exchanges some passionate screen kisses with Douglas, but she is arm-twisted to leave both Paris and the crestfallen Douglas behind. At the end of the movie, they are reunited outside Russia through scheming by Douglas.

Though today not remembered as a star for the ages, Douglas was a Hollywood headliner when "Ninotchka" was made, known as both a handsome leading man as well as being deft with light comedy. The winner of two acting Oscars for other movies, he captivated audiences with his handsome appearance, light mustache and liquid eyes. Douglas and Garbo starred together in three films.

The 1939 MGM release of "Ninotchka" is as much a political satire as romance because it relentlessly zings gallows humor at communist Russia with references to political purges and the ruthless secret police. Garbo delivers some of the topical laughs, such as her earnest summary of events in Moscow when greeted by Soviet colleagues in Paris, "The last mass trials were a great success. There are going to be fewer but better Russians."

1939
Ninotchka

Directed by ERNST LUBITSCH

Starring: GRETA GARBO (Nina Ivanovna Yakushova "Ninotchka") MELVYN DOUGLAS (Conte Leon d'Algout)
BELA LUGOSI / INA CLAIRE

Music by WERNER R. HEYMANN

ON A GOVERNMENT BUSINESS TRIP TO PARIS IN THE 1930S, A BOLSHEVIK OFFICIAL, PORTRAYED BY GRETA GARBO, FINDS HERSELF TEMPTED BY SOME OF CAPITALISM'S BOURGEOISIE PLEASURES THAT HER COMPANION MELVYN DOUGLAS SERVES UP WITH GUSTO. DOUGLAS PORTRAYS A PLAYBOY SMITTEN BY HIS BEAUTIFUL BUT RIGID RUSSIAN COMPANION, AND HAS MORE THAN AFFAIRS OF STATE ON HIS MIND WHEN THEY MEET IN PARIS.

▶

With a fast-paced stream of such dry humor, the movie represents Garbo's first comedy role, which at the time was marketed as "Garbo laughs!", coming nine years after famously being promoted with "Garbo talks!" in her first talking picture. Garbo received an Oscar nomination for "Ninotchka," which was one of three in her career. She never won for a performance, although she did receive a career achievement Oscar in 1955.

Garbo was born Greta Lovisa Gustafsson, in Sweden and her Scandinavian accent was a natural fit for her role as a Russian. At age 36, she cut her real-life screen legend short by abruptly abandoning Hollywood while still popular, in favor of a secluded life in New York, where she died in 1990. "Ninotchka" was her next to last film. The enigmatic actress never married and is famous for pursuing a life of frugality, and privacy, rejecting the pomp of a Hollywood star.

The movie certainly didn't seem particularly promising when being made. A black-and-white World War II propaganda film from Hollywood, the love-triangle melodrama serves as a springboard for a labored parable about patriotism and cynicism in wartime. During production, the screenplay was frantically re-written. Amazingly, from those inauspicious origins, "Casablanca" became a cinematic masterpiece that is on most lists of the Top 10 films of all time.

Humphrey Bogart portrays a night club owner in Nazi-controlled French Morocco, whose lost love—played by Ingrid Bergman—unexpectedly walks back into his life. But she's now married to another man, played by Paul Henreid, who seems more admirable than the world-weary Bogart. Yet the heart of Bergman's character is clearly torn.

All the characters of "Casablanca" seem doomed—with World War II raging in nearby Europe—and most appear to be engaged in some unsavory activity. The audience is left to root for the star-crossed former lovers Bergman and Bogart who, after being re-united early in the movie, manage to avoid the tragedy to which the storyline seems to propel them.

The movie won three Oscars in 1942, including Best Picture and Best Screenplay, and was nominated in five other categories. Bogart received one of the three Oscar acting nominations of his career (he one once) for his performance in "Casablanca."

"Casablanca" elevated Bergman—an accomplished Swedish and European film star fairly new to America at the time—to Hollywood's A-list, and a storied career with seven Oscar nominations in later roles (and three wins). The movie also altered the career of Bogart, who was already on the A-list actor, from being type-cast in Bad Guy roles by proving that audiences also accepted him as a romantic leading man.

"Casablanca's" visuals contribute to its timeless appeal, with an art deco flavor that is sleek and without excessive ornamentation that might date the Warner Bros. release. Characters dash around in stylishly simple, yet sophisticated European fashions. The North African architecture is uncluttered and punctuated by round, plain arches to frame scenes. In reality, "Casablanca" was filmed mostly in and around the Warner Bros. film studio lot in Burbank, California.

1942

Casablanca

Directed by MICHAEL CURTIZ

Starring: HUMPHREY BOGART (Rick Blaine) INGRID BERGMAN (Ilsa Lund)
PAUL HENREID / CLAUDE RAINS / CONRAD VEIDT

Music by M.K. JEROME / JACK SCHOLL / MAX STEINER

THE CHAOS OF WORLD WAR II'S EARLY DAYS SNAPPED A ROMANCE BETWEEN INGRID BERMAN AND HUMPHREY BOGART. THOUGH THEY STILL HAVE FEELINGS FOR EACH OTHER, THEY ARE UNEASY WHEN THEY MEET AGAIN IN NAZI-CONTROLLED CASABLANCA.

After their ill-fated romance, Humphrey Bogart and Ingrid Bergman are reunited by accident at Bogart's Casablanca bar. When Bogart asks piano player Dooley Wilson (seated) to "Play it again, Sam," it's for "As Time Goes By," their special song.

Despite frantic script re-writing during production, the movie overflows with immortal dialog that can be recited from memory by generations of cinema fans: From the heartrending love story, there's the tragic observation "With the whole world crumbling, we pick this time to fall in love," a working-through-the-pain plea to "Play it again, Sam," "If she can stand it, I can; Play it!" and a hopeful farewell toast, "Here's looking at you, kid."

In a welcome counterpoint to the serious and dark romantic plot, a stream of clever lines spring from political intrigues such as "Round up the usual suspects," "I'm shocked, shocked" (that there's gambling) and, finally, the question, "The waters? What waters? We're in the desert!" to which a deadpan Bogart responds, "I was misinformed."

When Bergman looks brokenheartedly at Bogart and begs, "Kiss me. Kiss me as if it were the last time," as Paris falls to the Nazis, it's hard for audiences around the world not to weep.

« - Ilsa: Play it once, Sam.
For old times' sake.
- Sam: I don't know what you mean, Miss Ilsa.
- Ilsa: Play it, Sam.
Play "As Time Goes By." »

In one of cinema's most classic scenes, star-crossed lovers (from far right) Ingrid Bergman and Humphrey Bogart arrive at a foggy airport in Casablanca where the authorities complicate plans to escape. ▶

The rags-to-riches folk tale about Cinderella is a world-famous story, with versions claimed by numerous other cultures. Though based on a universal tale about a hard-working but unappreciated young woman who suddenly gets recognition, Walt Disney's full-length animated "Cinderella" has been the world's reference point for this renowned story since 1950.

"A dream is a wish your heart makes," sings Cinderella character early in the musical romance movie. "No matter how your heart is grieving. If you keep on believing, the dream that you wish will come true." She is a pretty, blue-eyed young woman with a good heart and who tries to be cheerful, but her life is made miserable by her step-mother and two step-sisters.

Like all Disney animated features, "Cinderella" has some mildly-scary scenes. Just as a dressed up Cinderella is ready to go to a big dance at the king's palace, her two step sisters rip off her necklace and clothing in a frenzy when they realize that her outfit is made with their discarded items.

"Why you little thief!" shrieks Drizella. "They are my beads. Give them here." This leaves Cinderella standing helplessly in horror and on the verge of crying as her beautiful dress is reduced to tattered rags. After the humiliation, Cinderella cries a river of tears, saying to herself as she sobs, "There's nothing left to believe in. Nothing."

"Nonsense, child," a voice out of nowhere replies. "If you'd lost all your faith, I couldn't be here."

It's Cinderella's Fairy Godmother, a jolly, elderly woman with magical powers who comes to the rescue. "Oh ho, come now," the Fairy Godmother tells Cinderella. "Dry those tears. You can't go to the ball looking like that."

Fairy Godmother transforms Cinderella clothing and provides a horse-drawn carriage, which sets the stage for a rendezvous with Prince Charming at the king's big dance that night. The tale eventually turns—famously—on a glass slipper that Cinderella accidently leaves behind when she hurriedly leaves the palace and the slipper is the only clue of her identity.

AFTER A WONDERFUL NIGHT AT A PALACE DANCE, CINDERELLA LEAVES IN A HURRY BEFORE A MAGIC SPELL THAT MADE HER PRESENTABLE WEARS OFF. SHE ACCIDENTLY LEAVES BEHIND A GLASS SLIPPER ON THE STAIRS, THE ONLY CLUE TO HER IDENTITY.

1950
Cinderella

Directed by CLYDE GERONIMI / WILFRED JACKSON / HAMILTON LUSKE

Music by PAUL J. SMITH E OLIVER WALLACE (music) /
MACK DAVID / JERRY LIVINGSTON / AL HOFFMAN (lyrics)

A DREAM IS A WISH YOUR HEART MAKES,
WHEN YOU'RE FAST ASLEEP ...

Cinderella is treated like a servant in her own house, but with help from her animal friends (at left) who include two hovering blue birds and helpful three mice, she manages to fashion an elegant dress for a night at the palace.

▶ They make quite a sight as Cinderella's step-mother Lady Tremaine (from right) struts with her daughters Drizella and Anastasia. The daughters think they'll be the belles of the ball at the palace, but they underestimate the power of true love.

1

1. As Cinderella and her mouse friends watch in amazement, her Fairy Godmother conjures up a magic spell that will turn an ordinary garden pumpkin into a fine carriage.

2. It's love at first sight for Prince Charming when Cinderella appears at the palace grand ball and they dance the night away.

2 ▲

In dreams you will lose your heartaches, whatever you wish for you keep.

To enable the rendezvous with destiny, friendly mice struggle mightily to lift a key step-by-step up a long stairway to an imprisoned Cinderella so she can unlock a door to escape. The mice (who speak in squeaky, high-pitch voices), wild birds, house pets and barnyard animals are Cinderella's friends, providing a set of minor characters—each with a distinct personality. For example, a mouse named Gus is stocky and pugnacious, while a thin mouse Jacques is resourceful in outwitting the lazy and nasty house cat, Lucifer.

The 1 hour, 14 minute movie received three Oscar nominations in 1950—for Best Song, Best Scoring and Best Sound. The actors voicing the movie were not world famous, though some have interesting backgrounds. Prince Charming tunes were sung by a young Mike Douglas, who would later gained national fame as a daytime talk/variety TV show host. The opening narration was read by Betty Lou Gerson, who would voice the villain Cruella De Vil in Disney's "101 Dalmatians" 11 years later.

While praised, "Cinderella" gets some knocks. Some criticize Prince Charming—who only makes an impact late in the movie—for being bland, and find it jarring that he falls in love with Cinderella so quickly. Also, the film gets knocked for supposedly equating physical beauty with good-ness (and unattractiveness with evil). That judgment seems too harsh, because after all, this is a simple fairy tale, and most audiences want a hero-ine who is pretty and unambiguous.

But clearly the movie withstood the test of time because in 2002 and 2007, Disney released separate original animated direct-to-videos based on the Cinderella character.

▲ 1

When "Cinderella" was released in 1950, Walt Disney Studios was experiencing financial difficulties. Fortunately, "Cinderella" became a hit, allowing the then-struggling Disney studio to regain stability. Without "Cinderella," the Disney we know today would not have been able to achieve its continued greatness.

2

... HAVE FAITH IN YOUR DREAMS AND SOMEDAY
YOUR RAINBOW WILL COME SMILING THROUGH
NO MATTER HOW YOUR HEART IS GRIEVING
IF YOU KEEP ON BELIEVING THE DREAM THAT
YOU WISH WILL COME TRUE.

1. A glass slipper fits on Cinderella's dainty foot, which proves to the king's representative that Cinderella is the mysterious young woman who enchanted Prince Charming at the palace ball. Dressed in servant's clothing, Cinderella is an unlikely princess-to-be.

2. Prince Charming and Cinderella descend the vast stairs at the palace after their wedding, which marks the start of Cinderella's new life—as a princess. In a sign of true fairy-tale love, the prince does not care that Cinderella comes from humble origins.

Fate brings their characters together in "The African Queen," but Humphrey Bogart and Katharine Hepburn hate each other...at first.

Bogart portrays an ill-mannered, Canadian boat captain navigating the wild rivers of German East Africa in 1914, when World War I breaks out. He is then thrust on a perilous journey on his dilapidated 30-foot boat, which is named The African Queen, with a British missionary played by Hepburn—who is the prim and proper polar opposite of Bogart's slovenliness.

As they clash early in the film, Bogart cruelly lashes out, "Well, I ain't sorry no more, you crazy, psalm-singing, skinny old maid!"

The dangers and struggles of travelling the river while hiding from German soldiers gives them an appreciation of one another's strengths and gradually brings them together. In a scene famous for sickening audiences over the decades, Hepburn removes leeches from Bogart's body by applying salt after Bogart is forced to walk in the river shallows to pull the boat by a rope. "The filthy little devils," Bogart moans of the leeches.

When their cramped boat is moored in a pleasant section of river festooned with beautiful flowers and scents, their passion erupts, though the film is not explicit. "Aah, pinch me, Rosie," a giddy Bogart tells Hepburn after they unite. "Here we are going down the river like Antony and Cleopatra on their barge. If hadn't been for you, this couldn't be."

In what is a difficult feat, "The African Queen" combines drama, romance, comedy and high adventure—because their goal is to blow up a German gunboat at a lake that the river flows into.

Bogart won the Best Actor Oscar for the 1951 release, which is his only Academy Award win from three nominations in his storied career. The full-color "The African Queen" was nominated in three additional Oscars—all in major categories—leading actress for Hepburn, screenplay and director for John Huston. In her career, Hepburn won four Oscars from 12 nominations.

1951
The African Queen

Directed by JOHN HUSTON

Starring: HUMPHREY BOGART (Charlie Allnut)   KATHARINE HEPBURN (Rose Sayer)
ROBERT MORLEY / PETER BULL / THEODORE BIKEL

Music by ALLAN GRAY

IMMEDIATELY AFTER WORLD WAR I BREAKS OUT, AFRICAN RIVER BOAT CAPTAIN HUMPHREY BOGART AND UNLIKELY PASSENGER KATHARINE HEPBURN ARE FORCED INTO EACH OTHER'S LIVES TO DODGE GERMAN MILITARY. THEY SLEEP OUT IN BACKWATERS TO ESCAPE DETECTION.

Katharine Hepburn stands on to Bogart's shoulders while holding on to the mast of the African Queen river boat as they struggle to navigate a river on a perilous journey in German controlled East Africa in 1914.

Humphrey Bogart and Katharine Hepburn pull the African Queen river boat through a thick growth of reeds. Though they are complete opposites, they come to appreciate each other's strengths.

Director, writer and occasional actor Huston, who was nominated for 15 Oscars in his long career, also directed "The Maltese Falcon," "The Treasure of Sierra Madre" and "Key Largo"—all starring Bogart as well. The late Huston is the father of Oscar-winning actress Anjelica Huston.

Though possessing all the hallmarks of a major studio Hollywood picture, "The African Queen" was actually independently co-produced by United Artists (for the U.S. rights) and a British company, and filmed on location in Africa and at a studio in London. Being outside the studio system meant "The African Queen" wasn't automatically subjected to the then-strict Hollywood studio code mandating on-screen morality, allowing the suggestion that two unmarried lead characters are physical lovers.

"Dear Lord, we've come to the end of our journey," Hepburn prays aloud in a poignant moment when marooned and certain she will die with Bogart in the jungle, "and in a little while we will stand before you....Judge us not for our weakness, but for our love and open the doors of heaven for Charlie and me."

KR 12 6719 7676 •   -△- KR 12 6719 7676 •   -△- KR 12 6719 7676 •

«-Charlie (Humphrey Bogart):
Then, too, with me, it's always: 'Put things off. Never do today what you can put off till tomorrow.'-»

At first Katharine Hepburn and Humphrey Bogart simply want to avoid capture as World War I erupts, but then they hatch a plan to become marine saboteurs in what becomes a high adventure. They show grit, ingenuity and a growing fondness for each other.

Hollywood takes an idolized and humorous view of Ireland and romance in "The Quiet Man," which is a full-color movie released in 1952.

John Wayne portrays a burly man who arrives in the small Irish village of Innisfree in the 1930s, ostensibly as just another vacationing American, but then he reveals it's his birthplace that he left as a small boy. Wayne immediately falls for a red-haired beauty played by Maureen O'Hara, but discovers that Ireland has traditions that are foreign to him.

When Wayne dates O'Hara, they are chaperoned by a taxi driver whose conveyance is a horse-drawn buggy and who is portrayed by accomplished Irish actor Barry Fitzgerald. He had won the Oscar for Best Actor a few years earlier for "Going My Way."

"I don't get this," Wayne complains to Fitzgerald while on a date. "Why do we have to have you along? Back in the States, I'd drive up, honk the horn and the gal'd come running."

A keeper of Irish traditions, O'Hara is scandalized. "Come a-runnin'?" O'Hara repeats out loud in disbelief. "I'm no woman to be honking at and come a-runnin'."

But it's clear she has feelings for Wayne, and only her bullying brother, portrayed by Victor McLaglen, stands in their way. McLaglen would receive an Oscar nomination for his performance in the film.

"The Quiet Man" presents a romantic view of the Irish as quirky people with a penchant for gabbing, drinking, humor and fist-fights that are almost always friendly. The 2 hour, 9 minute color movie serves up numerous amusing Irish phrases such as "me throat's gone dry" and "is this a courtin' or a donnybrook?"—referencing a courtship that's becomes quarrelsome.

The film's title is also something of a joke given Wayne's tempestuous relationship with O'Hara and her two-fisted brother. "Well, he's a nice, quiet, peace-loving man, come home to Ireland to forget his troubles," Fitzgerald tells other curious locals and then adds this exaggeration: "He's a millionaire, you know, like all the Yanks."

1952
The Quiet Man

Directed by JOHN FORD

Starring: JOHN WAYNE (Sean Thornton)   MAUREEN O'HARA (Mary Kate Danaher)
VICTOR MCLAGLEN / BARRY FITZGERALD / Ward Bond

Music by VICTOR YOUNG

THEY'RE BOTH IRISH, SO OF COURSE TEMPERS FLARE. JOHN WAYNE PORTRAYS AN AMERICAN OF IRISH DESCENT WHO RETURNS TO THE SMALL VILLAGE IN IRELAND THAT HE LEFT AS A WEE CHILD. THERE HE WEDS THE HIGH-SPIRITED MAUREEN O'HARA, AND THE CULTURAL AND MARITAL MISUNDERSTANDINGS ENSUE.

The affectionate view of Ireland comes from acclaimed Hollywood director John Ford, who is famous for his American Westerns and who made more than a dozen films with Wayne. That affection can be attributed to both of Ford's parents being born in Ireland. The Ford-Wayne collaboration started with "Stagecoach" in 1939 and carried into the 1960s with "How the West Was Won." In fact, Wayne, O'Hara and McLaglen worked with Ford just a year earlier on the Western "Rio Grande."

For "The Quiet Man," most of the outside shots were filmed on location in Ireland, while the interiors and some exteriors were done in Hollywood. The location shoot was a family affair because Wayne brought his children, who are in the film (two of his kids exchange dialog with O'Hara when seated on a wagon during a horse race).

Maureen O'Hara and John Wayne want permission to engage in a courtship, as is the custom in 1930s Ireland, but O'Hara's brother Victor McLaglen (seated) makes life difficult. Barry Fitzgerald is a local Irish villager who oversees the courtship to make sure everything is proper and hands-off between O'Hara and Wayne.

76-77 John Wayne (on his back) gets flattened by a punch to his chin on his wedding day leaving his new wife, portrayed by Maureen O'Hara, and two wedding guests to revive him.

« –Michaleen Flynn:
I don't suppose there's a drop of anything wet in the house?
–"Red" Will Danaher:
Help yourself to the buttermilk.
–Michaleen Flynn:
Buttermilk! The Borgias would do better.–»

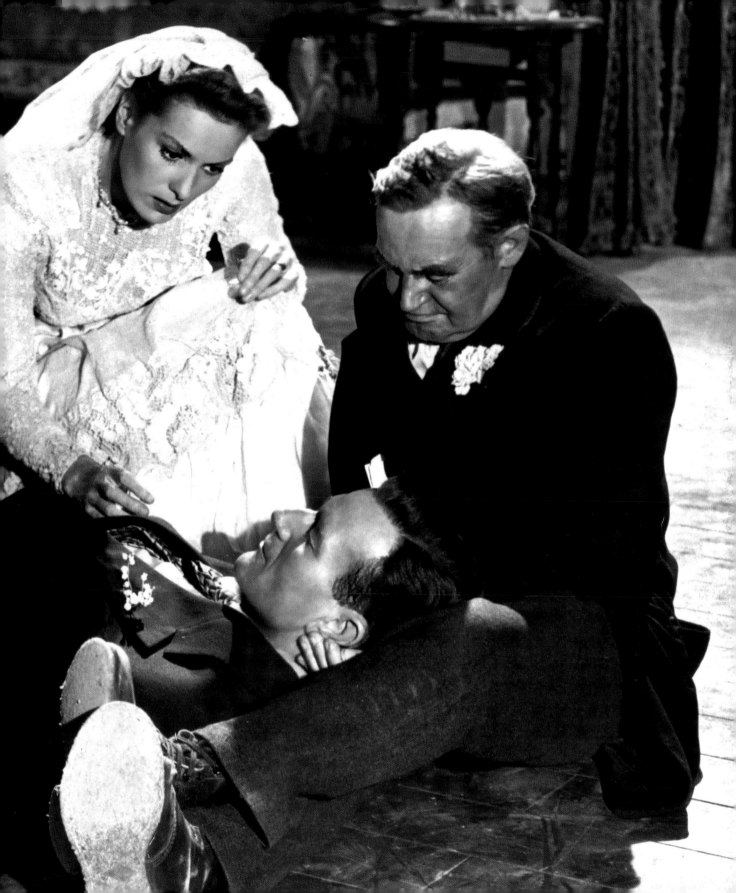

« - **Sean Thornton**: She isn't married or anything?
- **Michaleen Oge Flynn**: Married? That one? Not likely.
And her with her freckles and her temper...Oh, that red head of hers is no lie.
Still, a man might put up with that but not with her lack of a fortune. -»

1. A squabble over in-laws results in John Wayne spending his wedding night alone in sleeping bag, though his new bride Maureen O'Hara feels a little guilty in the morning. Wayne is an American who moves to Ireland in the 1930s for a quiet retirement that turns out to be anything but that.

2. American steel work worker and former boxer John Wayne seeks a quiet retirement in the small Irish village where he was born and instead he hooks up with Maureen O'Hara. Wayne tips his cap to the local clergy.

Critics find some weaknesses in the film. They see an over-the-top sentimentality about Ireland, Wayne's immediate marriage ambition seems too rushed, and O'Hara's portrayal of an excessively-reserved character who is overly anxious in the beginning of the film was called unrealistic.

Though the film is suitable for general audiences, some are also turned off by scenes of Wayne roughly dragging around O'Hara in public and once violently kicking down a bedroom door—which presumably viewers should chalk up to their Irish tempers boiling over.

"The Quiet Man" was distributed by independent B-film outfit Republic Pictures where Wayne was under contract, rather than one of Hollywood's seven major studios. Republic was noted for low-cost, simplistic shoot-em-up Westerns.

With Ford's A-list directing skills, Republic got two unaccustomed dividends from "The Quiet Man." The movie was a box office hit and it received seven Academy Award nominations, including Best Picture. Out of those seven, Ford won the Oscar for Best Director and the film also took in Best Cinematography, for which its full-color location shots in the Emerald Isle no doubt helped its cause.

"Roman Holiday's" position in cinema history is a matter of debate today. Some waive off the 1953 romantic comedy as just an elaborate travelogue in which the city of Rome is a co-star, with admittedly-gorgeous scenes framed by famous fountains, churches, palaces and the Coliseum (the Paramount release was filmed entirely in the Italian capital).

But others argue that "Roman Holiday" is an immortal classic because it made Audrey Hepburn a star, was nominated for 10 Oscars including Best Picture and today has rabid fans in unlikely places, such as Japan.

Hepburn portrays a European princess, and the British-born actress looks the part with her delicate angular facial features and toothpick body, which was a sharp contrast to the curvy Hollywood stars of that era. In the movie, Hepburn escapes the suffocating duties of European royalty by fleeing into the streets of Rome, where she accidently lands in the care of Gregory Peck—who portrays a layabout journalist.

"I've never been alone with a man before—even with my dress on," a woozy and seemingly drunk Hepburn tells Peck as she begins unbuttoning her blouse in his apartment when she is about to collapse. Peck, who finds her sleeping on the street, doesn't realize she's a newsworthy princess who is actually shaking off ill effects of a medical sedative. "With my dress off, it's *most* unusual," a tipsy Hepburn continues, almost pleased with her royally-improper behavior. "I don't seem to mind. Do you?"

Peck doesn't make romantic advances, although once he figures out that she's a famous princess on a lark he quickly schemes to milk his access into a money-making news story exposé that is certain to embarrass Hepburn.

PRINCESS-ON-THE-RUN AUDREY HEPBURN AND AMERICAN NEWSPAPERMAN GREGORY PECK EMBRACE WHILE DANCING IN ROME IN THE EARLY 1950S. SHE WANTS TO EXPERIENCE ROMAN LIFE FROM THE PERSPECTIVE OF AN ORDINARY PERSON, FREE FROM THE FORMALITIES OF ROYALTY AND RESTRICTIONS OF COURT LIFE.

1953
Roman Holiday

Directed by WILLIAM WYLER

Starring: GREGORY PECK (Joe Bradley)   AUDREY HEPBURN (Princes Ann, Anya Smith)
EDDIE ALBERT / HARTLEY POWER / HARCOURT WILLIAMS / MARGARET RAWLINGS

Music by GEORGES AURIC / VICTOR YOUNG

«-Princess Ann:
... Mr. Bradley, if you don't mind
my saying so, I think you are a ringer. -»

They spend a whirlwind 24-hours together that includes a wild ride on a motor scooter through the streets and alleys of Rome that lands them in traffic court. Peck gets them off by lying that they were just married.

Audiences can tell Hepburn is falling for Peck when she teases him after their court appearance that she won't make him marry her. "You don't have to look so worried. I won't hold you to it," she jokes and then adds with mock seriousness, "You don't have to be too grateful."

While Hepburn is enchanted, Peck is beginning to feel guilty about his deception, especially when she praises him for showing her Rome by saying, "I never heard of anybody so kind...also so completely unselfish." While Hepburn loves the carefree life of an ordinary person, she soon realizes that she's duty-bound to fulfill her role as a princess, which makes for a bitter-sweet final scene.

Originally, Peck was to be the only actor to receive star billing, but after production started he insisted he share top billing with Hepburn because he recognized that hers was a career-making performance. While Hepburn won the Oscar for Best Actress and supporting actor Eddie Albert was nominated, Peck—an established leading man—didn't even get nominated for Best Actor. But the role benefitted the handsome squared-jaw star with the authoritative baritone voice, by getting Hollywood to accept him in light comedy at a time when he was getting type-cast in dramas.

Gregory Peck drives a motor scooter in 1950s Rome while Audrey Hepburn hangs on. She portrays a European princess who has a runaway from the stifling obligations of royalty.

- Ann:
At midnight, I'll turn into a pumpkin
and drive away in my glass slipper.
- Joe:
And that will be the end of the fairy tale

2 ▲

1. Yup, it's her allright! Gregory Peck compares a photo of a missing European princess to a young woman he found lost on the street with no where to go.

2. They had fun romping in Rome when she was incognito, but now Audrey Hepburn's character is back to her royal duties. She is thankful that her indiscretion was not splashed in the news by her short-term companions (from left) Gregory Peck and Eddie Albert.

The famous Cinderella story as a comedy? "Sabrina" is that and more. The black-and-white movie from 1954 adds a pinch of drama and a heavy dose of star power with Audrey Hepburn, Humphrey Bogart and William Holden.

Hepburn, who portrays the daughter of a chauffer living on a sprawling estate home in suburban Long Island, N.Y., has a crush on one of the sons of her father's wealthy employer. But as a resident of the estate's servants' quarters, Hepburn can only watch from a distance.

"Don't reach for the moon, child," cautions John Williams, who portrays Hepburn's dignified and class-conscious chauffer father. He and Hepburn are both British with English accents in a movie filled with Americans. As "Sabrina" unfolds, it is explained that a British chauffer is necessary to maintain the small fleet of expensive European imports owned by the rich family.

Hepburn's heart-throb is Holden, who lives in the big house across the driveway, although he's a shameless playboy. In "Sabrina's" opening narration, Hepburn tells the audience with dry humor that Holden "went through several of the best eastern colleges for short periods of time, and through several marriages for even shorter periods of time."

The scandalous conduct of Holden provides plenty of comedy and the Cinderella storyline surfaces when geeky teenager Hepburn returns, completely transformed by a fashion and hair makeover, from a two-year stay at a Parisian school for chefs. Her personality also changes from shy schoolgirl to warm and self-confident sophisticate.

Holden revels at being Hepburn's long-wanted love, telling his brother, portrayed by Bogart, "Isn't it amazing? Would you have recognized her?" marvels Holden, who was slacked jawed when he first realized moments earlier that the sophisticated beauty is the chauffer's daughter. "That scrawny little kid who used to whip around corners every time she saw us coming."

The drama heats up when the audience is left to wonder if Bogart intentionally side-lines his brother Holden to monopolize Hepburn's attention. She begins to like Bogart, finding humanity behind his façade as the workaholic who runs his family's giant business.

▶ HUMPHREY BOGART IS ONE OF TWO BROTHERS WHO ARE IN A GROWING COMPETITION FOR AUDREY HEPBURN. AT THIS PARTICULAR MOMENT, IT IS BOGART WHO HAS CORNERED HEPBURN'S AFFECTIONS.

1954
Sabrina

Directed by BILLY WILDER

Starring: HUMPHREY BOGART (Linus Larrabee) AUDREY HEPBURN (Sabrina Fairchild)
WILLIAM HOLDEN / JOHN WILLIAMS

Music by FREDERICK HOLLANDER

▲ 1

When Bogart's father tells him to pay off Hepburn to get her to leave, Bogart defends her. "She doesn't want money," Bogart says. "She wants love...the last of the romantics."

The climax is a three-way puzzle. Will Hepburn go for Holden, assuming he promises to settle down, or Bogart, for whom a wife would require cutting back on an obsession with work? Holden comes to understand he has competition for Hepburn's affections, and the audience is left to see whether he or Bogart will seize the initiative and elbow the other to woo Hepburn.

Hepburn is the perfect image of a woman first seen on the screen as a teenager—her slim body accented by a pencil-thin waist line—who later is transformed. While Hepburn is believable, some criticize "Sabrina's" other casting, suggesting that Holden and particularly Bogart look too old to be credible suitors for the girlish Hepburn. Some also complain that a half-hearted suicide attempt by one character early on is also out of place in what is mostly a light romantic comedy.

«-Sabrina Fairchild:

If you should have any difficulty recognizing your daughter, I shall be the most sophisticated woman at the Glen Cove station. -»

1. At a Parisian cooking school, Audrey Hepburn stands for inspection of her soufflé. The chef starts with her colleague, the Barron, who convinces Hepburn to adopt Parisian glamour in her wardrobe.

2. When the chauffer's daughter portrayed by Audrey Hepburn returns a sophisticate from Paris, William Holden doesn't immediately recognize her as the tomboy who lived in the servants' quarters of his family's estate in the New York City suburbs.

Legendary Hollywood costume designer Edith Head won the Oscar for dressing Hepburn, which is the only Academy Award win among six nominations for "Sabrina." Hepburn received a nomination as Lead Actress.

Credit for making "Sabrina" a hit goes to director Billy Wilder, whose behind-the-camera genius enabled the 1 hour, 53 minute movie to deftly mix comedy and drama. Wilder, who received two Oscar nominations for "Sabrina," would next direct Marilyn Monroe in the comedy "The Seven Year Itch". He won six Oscars in his career for directing and writing, and also a career achievement award.

The Paramount Pictures release was mostly filmed in Hollywood, though some outdoors scenes were shot in and around New York City. The sprawling and opulent mansion that is central to the film was then owned by Paramount chief Barney Balaban and is actually on Long Island, which is the suburb where the film's story takes place.

1. Audrey Hepburn is surprised when Humphrey Bogart, and not his brother, meets her in the deserted tennis court at his palatial estate while a big party goes on at the main house.

2. In the 1950s two brothers, portrayed by William Holden and Humphrey Bogart, become rivals for the heart of Audrey Hepburn in a wealthy enclave just outside of New York City.

«-Oliver Larrabee: I only hope you remember what to do with a girl. -»
«-Linus Larrabee: It'll come back to me. It's like riding a bicycle. .-»

Though a decent person, Humphrey Bogart is ob-sessed with work with time for little else so he's an un-likely suitor for the fun-loving Audrey Hepburn. Meanwhile, Bogart's breezy brother (not seen) seems a better match for Hepburn.

Lady is a dog who leads a charmed life, until the woman of her house gets pregnant and the upheaval from adding a new baby makes the dog wonder if she is still wanted. Walt Disney Studios' full-length animated film "Lady and the Tramp" is an adventure story about loyalty, courage and redemption that answers Lady's doubts.

In "Lady and the Tramp's" cartoon world, dogs talk to each other, but not to humans. And dogs have personalities to fit their breed. For example, a Scottish terrier named Jock is voiced with a Scottish accent and conducts himself in a reserved, dignified manner.

When Lady is trying to understand the implications of adding a baby to her human family, her street-wise male dog friend Tramp only intensifies her fears. "Yeah, they scratch, pinch, pull ears," Tramp says of human babies. "Aw, but shucks, any dog can take that! It's what they do to your happy home...Home-wreckers...that's what they are!"

Aunt Sarah—who arrives with two devious Siamese cats—takes over temporarily at Lady's home, which drives her into the streets and to an unwanted adventure for which she is not suited.

Lady is an American cocker spaniel from a wealthy home—strutting and lifting up paws smartly while keeping her head held high. Disney animators fashioned Lady into a dog version of a "princess"—the young, dignified and beautiful female character that is a fixture of Disney animation stories. Lady has obvious feminine accents such as long fluffy ears and eyelashes.

Fortunately for Lady, her friend Tramp guides her through the perils of life on the street—which the movie portrays as both dangerous and exhilarating. When Tramp discovers that Lady has never chased chickens for fun, he coaxes her saying, "Ho, ho, then you've never lived!" adding that part of the joy is that dogs know it's wrong to do.

Tramp continues to talk up life "off the leash," but Lady is not convinced. "It sounds wonderful," Lady says weakly. "But who'd watch over the baby?"

Even rejection does not shake Lady's family loyalty, which is rewarded when she ends up back home with her owners and the new baby. And Tramp becomes more than just a guy pal.

1955
Lady and the Tramp

Directed by CLYDE GERONIMI / WILFRED JACKSON / HAMILTON LUSKE

Music by OLIVER WALLACE

TRAMP AND LADY ENJOY A ROMANTIC, CANDLE-LIT SPAGHETTI DINNER IN THE ALLEY BEHIND AN ITALIAN RESTAURANT. THE RESTAURANT'S GOOD-HEARTED WORKERS GIVE THE DOGS A FREE MEAL AND EVEN SERENADE THEM. WHEN LADY AND TRAMP GOBBLE UP OPPOSITE ENDS OF THE SAME STRING OF SPAGHETTI, THEIR SNOUTS PRESS TOGETHER ACCIDENTLY. THIS BIT OF PUPPY LOVE IS ONE OF CINEMA'S MOST MEMORABLE SCENES.

As in all Disney films, it's not all sweetness, though "Lady and the Tramp" is suitable for all audiences. When Lady is briefly held captive in the city's dog pound, dogs are shown crying tears and three sad puppies are huddled together. This sequence is lightened by a humorous chorale of dogs singing.

The most gripping is Tramp and Lady fighting a rat—seen mainly as two slanting menacing yellow eyes darting in dark-ness—when the rat gets into the bedroom of the baby at night.

The film's most famous scene presents Tramp and Lady eating opposite ends of a long single strand of spaghetti. When they both suck in their ends, their muzzles accidently come together as if kissing, putting a surprised and embarrassed look on Lady's face. In this scene, the two dogs are in an alley behind an Italian food restaurant where two workers regularly feed Tramp, and they set up a table with a candle when they see he has brought Lady.

After scary adventures on the run in the city and in the dog pound, Lady and Tramp settle down to a peaceful, happy life with a family of their own.

« -Gilda (Peggy Lee):
And I wish that I could travel his way, I wish that I could travel his way. »

Another memorable element is singing by big band and jazz vocalist Peggy Lee, who was an established recording star when the Disney movie came out in 1955. She voices several characters as well.

Among the movie's many charms is its dog's eye view of the world. When there's a party at her house, Lady is shown walking among a forest of long dresses and pants legs because the people around her are cut off at the waist.

"Lady and the Tramp" creates such a dog-centric world that the name of the pregnant woman in charge of Lady's household is unknown. Throughout the 1 hour, 15 minute-long movie, she is referred to only as "Darling" by her husband, who is called "Jim Dear" by the wife.

He's sure it's a love that will be durable and, though her heart says yes, she's conflicted in "Love is a Many-Splendored Thing."

The 1955 romantic drama stars William Holden as a brash American correspondent in Hong Kong who falls for co-star Jennifer Jones. She's the movie's complex character as a Eurasian woman—her late father was Chinese—who is left scarred by the death of her Chinese husband. Jones' character struggles to fit between two different cultures.

After a persistent Holden presses her for a dinner date, the demure Jones pushes back, saying her Chinese "third uncle would consider it unpardonable to accept. No Chinese girl would dare dine alone with an American she had just met...I am still Chinese."

"And half European," counters Holden."I just heard you say so. Now will your European side reconsider?" a triumphant Holden asks, looking obviously pleased that he has bent logic to favor his romantic overture. The Jones character is very Western, having returned to Asia after a decade studying medicine in England.

Jones' petite physique helps in shaping a Eurasian profile, and she is outfitted with Chinese accents like Oriental clothing and jet black hair. However, some critics complain that she isn't credible and movie's constant references to her character's Chinese ancestry are annoying. Western bigotry toward the Chinese and clannishness by the Chinese are central themes in the movie.

Other than that knock, "Love is a Many-Splendored Thing" is praised as one of the finest romantic dramas from the end of Hollywood's studio system era. In the 1950s, the passion on screen is limited to kisses, embraces and the implied but never sensual nudity, which would gradually become acceptable in the following decade.

But "Love is a Many-Splendored Thing" is not completely timid. The couple hurdles many obstacles to love, only to arrive at a truly sad ending. "I do not know what is to happen, darling," Holden writes while travelling to Jones. "But this I do know. Life's greatest tragedy is not to be loved."

"Love is a Many-Splendored Thing" received eight Oscar nominations for 1955, including Best Picture. But its three wins were secondary categories, including Best Song for the title track, which was a surprise hit in the U.S. music charts when the film came out.

This movie came towards the end of Jones' Hollywood career, providing her fifth and final Oscar nomination. Jones won the Oscar for Best Leading Actress more than a decade earlier for "The Song of Bernadette," which like this movie is directed by veteran Henry King. His many credits date well back into the silent film era.

1955
Love is a Many-Splendored Thing

Directed by HENRY KING

Starring: WILLIAM HOLDEN (Mark Elliott) **JENNIFER JONES** (Han Suyin)
TORIN THATCHER / ISOBEL ELSOM

Music by ALFRED NEWMAN

THE ROMANCE BETWEEN JENNIFER JONES AND WILLIAM HOLDEN IS TABOO BECAUSE THE JONES CHARACTER IS HALF CHINESE. BOTH WESTERN AND CHINESE SOCIETIES FROWNED ON INTERRACIAL LOVES IN THE MID 1950S.

While Holden did not get Oscar nominated for "Love is a Many-Splendored Thing," he was a towering Hollywood star at the time—receiving top billing. Holden had won an Academy Award for lead actor two years earlier for WWII prison drama "Stalag 17" and he would receive three Oscar nominations in his full career.

"Love is a Many-Splendored Thing" is set in the turbulent year of 1949, when mainland China was being taken over by communists while the British colony of Hong Kong—with its English and Chinese population—faced an uncertain future. The movie is based on a novel by Han Suyin and draws its name from verse by British poet Francis Thompson.

A third star of the film is the city-state of Hong Kong—the Asian metropolis exuding a restless energy that leaps up from the shores of a scenic bay framed by soaring hills and peaks. This gives "Love is a Many-Splendored Thing" a magnificent backdrop that is both urban and naturally beautiful.

20th Century Fox arranged for extensive location shooting in Hong Kong to achieve a rich on-location look in gorgeous full color. This was in part to counter the success of TV, that in the 1950s was draining audiences from cinemas with cheap in-studio programming.

A wealthy Newport, R.I. heiress, portrayed by Grace Kelly, is preparing for a large, posh wedding at her mansion, but there's a complication in "High Society." Her ex-husband, played by Bing Crosby, admits he's still in love with her. He lives next door and does his subtle best to undermine the pending nuptials.

"You'd be a wonderful woman if you'd just, just let your tiara slip a little," Crosby tells the aloof Kelly during a private moment in this musical romantic comedy from 1956.

"I wanted to say those first weeks we spent together were the most wonderful I've ever known," Crosby says of their marriage. "I want to thank you for them. Good luck."

When Crosby leaves Kelly, it's obvious she is torn by self-doubt, which intensifies when her fiancée, portrayed by John Lund, appears. The fiancée—who is a wealthy and stiff businessman—tries to be soothing, telling Kelly she's like "a statue to be worshipped" and that he'll put her on a "pedestal...where I can look up and adore you." This unnerves Kelly even more, because it unwittingly takes cues from Crosby's criticism that she's cold and remote. Crosby's character is a breezy, fun-loving song writer. Kelly is an aristocratic beauty whose classic good looks enchant men. She impresses women, too, with her shapely figure, sleek, well-coiffed hair and air of sophistication.

"High Society" turns up the improbable but amusing comedy when Kelly gets drunk the night before her wedding and falls for a scandal magazine reporter, played by Frank Sinatra. Sinatra is covering Kelly's wedding with a photographer, played by Celeste Holm, who has her own romantic ambitions for Sinatra.

In the morning, Kelly is left to sort out her indiscretions of the night before, which are foggy except that various people tell her about her embarrassing behavior at different points of the evening. "Oh, I'm such an unholy mess of a girl," Kelly says with downcast eyes to an understanding Crosby.

FREE SPIRITED AND FUN-LOVING, BING CROSBY IS AT SEA ON HIS SAIL BOAT WITH ON-AND-OFF FLAME PORTRAYED BY GRACE KELLY, WHO'S STUFFY AND RESERVED PERSONALITY IS THE OPPOSITE OF HIS.

1956
High Society

Directed by CHARLES WALTERS

Starring: BING CROSBY (C.K. Dexter-Haven) GRACE KELLY (Tracy Samantha Lord)
FRANK SINATRA / CELESTE HOLM / LOUIS ARMSTRONG / JOHN LUND

Music by COLE PORTER

«-Louis Armstrong:
He's gonna get nowhere with that kind of music. Good for the feet, nothin' for the heart.-»

The wedding is on, but the audience is left to guess who the groom will be: the fiancée, old flame Crosby or new flame Sinatra?

Besides those big stars, the MGM release sports a solid supporting cast that includes trumpet jazz legend Louis Armstrong and his band, whose are in town for the Newport Jazz Festival that is a backdrop element of the movie. Armstrong, Crosby, Sinatra and Kelly sing, making "High Society" a musical in addition to romantic comedy.

"High Society" was nominated for Oscars in two musical categories. Crosby, Kelly, Sinatra and Holm were already Oscar-winning actors when the film came out.

"High Society" actually combines two film projects. It's a remake of "The Philadelphia Story" from 1940, starring Katharine Hepburn and Cary Grant that was fused with a musical called "Jazz in Newport."

Released in the mid 1950s, "High Society" contains dated period elements including fashion (including two-tone men's "wing-tip" shoes) and reference to "Spy" magazine whose cover price is 15 cents and is read in barber shops. But other elements play timelessly, such as Kelly toying with reporters Sinatra and Holm when they first meet, making seemingly-innocent conversation that Kelly slyly turns into pointed barbs.

Asking Sinatra and Holm if they have a romantic thing going, they are momentarily embarrassed. "It's the sort of the intimate little detail that you like to write about, isn't it?" Kelly asks the two tabloid reporters, who make their living being intrusive. "Oh, but if you'd rather not have your privacy invaded, I will certainly respect your wishes."

Later, Kelly delivers this mocking compliment to Holm's hairdo, "It's lovely," Kelly says with a straight face. "Is it lacquered?"

When "High Society" was filmed, Kelly was in the process of leaving Hollywood for her storybook wedding to Prince Rainer of Monaco. This was her last Hollywood movie.

Grace Kelly could have her choice between ex-husband Bing Crosby (left) or the new-man in her life Frank Sinatra. The setting is the Newport Jazz Festival so music legend Louis Armstrong is on hand with his trumpet.

«-Bing Crosby:
...... act naturally-»

Marilyn Monroe desperately wanted to be taken seriously by the New York cultural elite, so she insisted on starring in several films with a darker side, including "Bus Stop." She did so over objections of studio executives at 20th Century Fox and to a lukewarm response from audiences, who preferred her playing the ditzy blonde in purely silly comedies.

So at the height of her stardom in 1956, Marilyn portrayed a pathetic saloon singer trapped in a depressing, dead-end life with "Bus Stop." The romantic drama-comedy is based on a hit Broadway stage play that was praised by the New York cultural elite and provided the dramatic scenes that Monroe craved.

"I just want to tell you something," she stammers in a weepy scene where she haltingly admits to a suitor that her past is not pure. "It's kind of personal and embarrassing too, but I ain't the kind of girl you thought I was. Well, I guess a lot of people would say I've had a real wicked life and I guess I have too."

Earlier, after being berated by a saloon keeper, Monroe is distraught saying, "He called me an ignorant hillbilly." Then she wells up her courage to say with conviction, "I've been trying to be somebody."

In addition to being a drama, "Bus Stop" has elements of romantic farce, which provide an excuse for Monroe to parade around in a revealing saloon-girl teddy outfit. This image of Monroe was used heavily to promote the film while its unappealing dark side was completely omitted. Her suitor—newcomer Don Murray—engages in entertaining, over-the-top antics by portraying a strapping Montana ranch lad in the big city for the first time, who immediately wants to marry Monroe.

"I come down for the rodeo tomorrow with the idea of finding me an angel. And you're it," says Murray, whose naiveté results in his in treating women little better than cattle. "Now, I don't have a lot of time for sweet talking."

In a climax at a roadside restaurant on the bus route from which the film draws its title, Monroe comes to appreciate the sincere and unspoiled Murray, and he soon figures out how to be more genteel toward her.

1956
Bus Stop

Directed by JOSHUA LOGAN

Starring: MARILYN MONROE (Cherie) DON MURRAY ("Bo" Decker)
ARTHUR O'CONNELL / BETTY FIELD / EILEEN HECKART

Music by ALFRED NEWMAN / CYRIL J. MOCKRIDGE

MARILYN MONROE SUPPORTS HERSELF AS A SALOON SINGER WHEN SHE CATCHES THE EYE OF COWBOY DON MURRAY, WHO IS IN TOWN FOR A RODEO ▲
COMPETITION AND TREATS WOMEN MUCH AS HE DOES CATTLE BACK AT THE RANCH.

Whenever Monroe turned in a fine acting performance for a film, movie critics would marvel—forgetting that they often had said the same thing before. "Hold onto your chairs, everybody," says a 1956 New York Times review of "Bus Stop," "because the little lady creates a real character in this film." In acting her part convincingly, Monroe adopted a authentic southern accent and sang with a sultry sexiness but—in what is very difficult—slightly off-key to accurately portray her untalented singer character.

But a reputation as a serious actress eluded Monroe in her cut-short life. She was never nominated for an Oscar in her entire career, despite repeatedly enchanting audiences with flawless and completely believable performances. Adding insult to injury in "Bus Stop," her male opposite—newcomer Murray—received an Academy Award nomination, which was the film's only Oscar honor.

Cary Grant plays a loveable scoundrel, famous around the world for brief flings, who falls in serious love with elegant beauty Deborah Kerr when she initially resists him in "An Affair to Remember." This sentimental road film, which is punctuated by frequent touches of humor, keeps audiences guessing whether Grant will wed another woman of great wealth or somehow end up with Kerr, either for a brief interlude of passion or perhaps for a lifetime.

In the 1957 release from 20th Century Fox, the world-wise Kerr is clever and self-assured, in what runs counter to most sympathetic Hollywood heroines of the era who depend on landing a man for happiness. "You've known quite a few (women) haven't you?" she playfully teases Grant over a meal. "Or perhaps 'few' is the wrong word...And I suppose they've all been madly in love with you....But you haven't had much respect for them."

A memorable scene occurs at the observation deck on the 86th floor of the Empire State Building in New York, where Kerr tells Grant to meet six months after they part. It's a test to see if they can detach from their other loves. But the appointment itself turns out to be fraught with complications that lead to another separation followed by a finale.

The film offers little hot passion on the screen, leaving the romance to be suggested by dialog and the longing from separation. "Let's not complicate it anymore," Kerr says while they agonize over their will-we-or-won't-we relationship. "I can think more clearly when you are not around. So you go think in your room and I'll think in mine—while we miss each other."

"An Affair to Remember" received four Oscar nominations, though none in acting or other major categories. The color-rich movie is a remake of 1939 black-and-white movie "Love Affair," which received six Oscar nominations. The two versions won no Oscars despite their combined 10 nominations. Both were directed by Leo McCarey, who won two Oscars for other films and whose career is noteworthy for helming mostly warm, sentimental films. "Love Affair" was again remade in 1994.

1957
An Affair to Remember

Directed by LEO MCCAREY

Starring: CARY GRANT (Nickie Ferrante) DEBORAH KERR (Terry McKay)
RICHARD DENNING / NEVA PATTERSON / CATHLEEN NESBITT

Music by HUGO FRIEDHOFER / HARRY WARREN

CARY GRANT AND DEBORAH CARR ARE ATTRACTED TO EACH OTHER WHEN THEY MEET ON A TRANS-ATLANTIC OCEAN LINER TRIP IN THE 1950S BUT BOTH HAVE OTHER OFF-SHIP ROMANCES IN THEIR LIVES. BACK IN NEW YORK CITY AFTER THEIR OCEAN VOYAGE, THE DURABILITY OF THEIR ROMANCE WILL BE TESTED. WILL THEY GO THEIR SEPARATE WAYS OR RE-UNITE?

But it's this bright 1957 version that is remembered, carried by the ageless appeal of Grant's smooth sophistication and likeability. And there's Kerr's elegantly-styled, short red hair, chiseled facial features and impeccable complexion that eliminates any need for those gauzy close-up required by some other Hollywood female stars. Both are British-born, though Kerr's speech mostly sounds American with just occasional hints of an English accent. Playing off each other, they improvised bits of humor that ended up in the final film.

"An Affair to Remember" isn't on everyone's favorite list. Some knock the film as being a superficial tear jerker that is over-dressed with oppressively bright-colored women's fashion of the era, and sequences with a children's choir that seems out of place.

But others revere "An Affair to Remember," which received a major homage in "Sleepless in Seattle" (see page 202) decades later. In that 1993 hit film starring Tom Hanks and Meg Ryan, film clips, music and dialog constantly celebrate "An Affair to Remember."

Six long years in the making, "Sleeping Beauty" is the last of the Walt Disney Studios full-length animated films to be completely hand drawn. Studio artists meticulously crafted 24 hand-drawn mini-paintings for every second of screen time in this 1 hour, 15 minute movie that premiered in theaters in 1959.

The movie masterpiece is also noteworthy as Disney's first full-length animated feature that is filmed in 70mm, a bigger film format that provides more richness than 35mm stock.

"Sleeping Beauty" has all the hallmarks of Disney's world-famous animation: a story set in a far-off realm, magic, intriguing characters, enchanting music and romance. Based on a European fairy tale, the movie is about the certainty of destiny and true love conquering all.

Princess Aurora—a pretty blonde with blue-eyes and a girlish figure—is bought up by three daffy fairy godmothers deep in a forest where she can only imagine what true love might be like. "Well, he's tall and handsome, and... and so romantic," Aurora says to the woodland animals that are her friends. "Oh, we walk together, and talk together, and just before we say goodbye, he takes me in his arms, and then... I wake up. Yes, it's only in my dreams."

Aurora has a brief, chance meeting with the prince before they realize their destinies are intertwined. But first, a spell must be broken, tears shed, an evil castle infiltrated and the prince rescued by the fairy godmothers: Flora, Fauna and Merryweather. The fairies fuss and frequently disagree with each other—sometimes resulting in comedy when they cast opposite spells on the same target—but they always work out amicable solutions.

The legendary studio founder Walt Disney understood his family animated films needed a spicy antagonist to drive the story and to provide a stark contrast to the protagonist's warmth. "Sleeping Beauty" is electrified by a diabolically wicked witch Maleficent, who is a relentless foe of fair Aurora.

1959

Sleeping Beauty

Directed by CLYDE GERONIMI / LES CLARK / ERIC LARSON / WOLFGANG REITHERMAN

Music by TOM ADAIR / GEORGE BRUNS

PRINCESS AURORA, WHO LIVES IN SECRECY AND SECLUSION IN THE FOREST TO ESCAPE AN EVIL PROPHESY, MADE FRIENDS WITH FOREST ANIMALS WHO MAGICALLY UNDERSTAND HER CONVERSATION. AS SHE WALKS ALONG, THE ADORING CRITTERS FOLLOW HER.

Maleficent has some great lines, some of which elicit chuckles from adults as well as kids: "What a pity Prince Phillip can't be here to enjoy the celebration," the queen of mean tells an evil sidekick in her castle. "Come, we must go to the dungeon and cheer him up."

At another juncture, she rails at her henchmen, "Fools! Idiots! Imbeciles!" After banishing them, she turns to a minion and says in exasperation, "Oh, they're hopeless. A disgrace to the forces of evil."

After playing large, issuing loud wicked laughs and casting a diabolical spell, the black-caped Maleficent who is in elegant human form but with two horns on her head, finds her evil plan quickly unravels at the end of the film. It takes just one kiss in a wordless scene to break her curse.

With animation anything is possible, and Disney animators conjure up truly imaginative sequences. Aurora sings a joyous song as she strolls through the forest accompanied by hovering birds, adorable rabbits and quizzical squirrels—who understand as she talks to them.

⌃ 1

◂ 2

1. As the queen holds her baby Princess Aurora in her arms, she counts on friendly magic from one of three fairy godmothers to ward off an evil spell from a sorceress.

2. The evil sorceress Maleficent is absolutely wicked to the core and has an army of followers at her castle, though she frequently rages about their incompetence in carrying out her orders.

1

When the good fairies have to do house cleaning, more animation magic ensues because just a wave of the magic wand is all that's needed. An animated bucket, mop and boom spiff up the place, all while seeming to dance across the room. Even the furniture moves itself. All this happens without any labor by the fairies.

When "Sleeping Beauty" was released in 1959, Disney let it be known that the hand-drawn film cost a then-hefty $6 million. While a risk, the movie proved to be a box office success and received one Oscar nomination—for best scoring of a musical picture.

"Sleeping Beauty," which is credited as Disney's 16th full-length animated feature, capped a decade during which the studio launched earlier animation triumphs in "Cinderella," "Alice in Wonderland," "Peter Pan" and "Lady and the Tramp."

2

1. The horn-headed Maleficent lures Princess Aurora into fulfilling a curse, which is assures the girl will die if she cuts her finger on a spinning wheel before her 16th birthday.

2. After he escapes from dungeon imprisonment, heroic Prince Phillip faces a fearsome dragon, as the forces of evil try to keep him from re-uniting with Princess Aurora and awaken her from her sleeping spell.

116-117 Only true love's kiss can lift the spell of a sorceress to awaken the sleeping beauty Princess Aurora from a permanent slumber.

In the early 1960s, Italian films took the center stage of world cinema with captivating movies critical of the decadence of the post-WWII economic boom. This movement broke with Italian cinema's celebrated neo-realism emphasizing poverty and rural themes, and emerged just before gritty Italian spaghetti Westerns would also enthrall the world.

The 1963 romantic comedy "Yesterday, Today and Tomorrow" ("Ieri, oggi e domani") explores the contemporary materialist society in a three-segment anthology—each starring Sophia Loren and Marcello Mastroianni. The Italian-language film won the Oscar for Best Foreign Film.

In the opening segment set in Naples, Loren is the streetwise breadwinner of her growing family but faces jail for selling contraband cigarettes. Only by being pregnant will she dodge jail time, and Mastroianni—her lazy, unemployed husband—must keep her constantly pregnant, which exhausts him.

"Dizzy spells. Wobbly legs," Mastroianni complains to his mother, citing symptoms that are usually associated with a pregnant woman. "If you must know, I've fainted twice in the street. And the more I become a wreck, the more she's at me."

Loren, who is frightened of going to jail, even considers seducing a neighbor when Mastroianni can't perform to conceive an eighth child, after a medical doctor says he needs rest. An unsympathetic Loren storms out of their apartment at one point, telling the pooped-out Mastroianni, "goodbye, sissy." It's another bit of humor that reverses the usual gender stereotypes.

Decadence in the upper class comes up big in the other two anthology segments. In the movie's most famous scene, Loren is a call girl in Rome and the wealthy Mastroianni is her mousy client, a government minister from an important family.

The signature scene of "Yesterday, Today and Tomorrow" shows Loren performing a seductive strip tease, starting in sexy black lingerie. Watching on the far end of the bed is a giddy Mastroianni, who at one point appreciatively howls like a wolf as his excitement builds with every piece of Loren's clothing that lands on the floor.

1963
Yesterday, Today and Tomorrow

Directed by VITTORIO DE SICA

Starring: SOPHIA LOREN (Adelina Sbaratti/Anna Molteni/Mara)
MARCELLO MASTROIANNI (Carmine Sbaratti/Renzo/Augusto Rusconi)
ALDO GIUFFRÉ / AGOSTINO SALVIETTI / ARMANDO TROVAJOLI / TINA PICA

Music by ARMANDO TROVAJOLI

TWO GIANTS OF ITALIAN CINEMA, MARCELLO MASTROIANNI AND SOPHIA LOREN PLAY THREE VERY DIFFERENT CHARACTERS IN THE THREE-PART ROMANTIC COMEDY "YESTERDAY, TODAY AND TOMORROW" ("IERI, OGGI E DOMANI").

A seductive strip-tease by Sophia Loren who portrays a call girl in Rome provides an erotic scene that Hollywood could not match in 1963 because the major studios enforced rules requiring on-screen morality. Those restrictions were swept away a few years later.

The strip-tease is voyeuristic delight, but just as Loren is about to take off her bra, she has second thoughts. Though a paying customer, Mastroianni gets frustrated by a succession of comic events. "Please, it turns me off if you laugh," Mastroianni says as he tries to undress Loren at one point. "This is serious."

"Yesterday, Today and Tomorrow" is also noteworthy for capturing the old Italy in its tattered glory before the post-WWII economic revival changed the urban landscape. That backdrop is in constant view in the third segment, which follows a Rolls Royce as it is driven around Milan. The luxury automobile is owned by Loren, who is a bored rich wife of a wealthy man, and she is romantically attracted to the earthy Mastroianni.

As a comedy, there's not a lot of passion in the 1 hour, 59 minute movie. Though Loren is sexually naughty in all three anthology segments, it's only the strip tease that is visually erotic (and was featured prominently in the promotional film trailer).

Marcello Mastroianni can barely contain his anticipation as Sophia Loren disrobes one piece of clothing at a time in her apartment in Rome. He's a meek government bureaucrat from an influential family and pays Loren for her services.

▲ 1

When the film came out, Loren was riding high from winning the Oscar for Best Actress two years earlier. Her sleek Mediterranean beauty, voluptuous body and acting skills made her the face of Italian cinema. Mastroianni is also a cinema giant who would receive three Oscar nominations for performances in other films.

In his career, director Vittorio De Sica had an impressive run with Hollywood-honored foreign films. In addition to "Yesterday, Today and Tomorrow," his acclaimed works also include "The Bicycle Thief" ("Ladri di biciclette"), "Shoeshine" ("Sciuscià") and "The Garden of the Finzi-Continis" ("Il giardino del Finzi-Contini").

For American audiences in 1963, a big appeal of Italian (and French) cinema was its frank presentation of passion and nudity, which was not permitted in Hollywood studio films. However, a screen morality code enforced by Hollywood's studios was abandoned by the late 1960s. This permitted more saucy U.S. films that cut into the sophisticated audience segment that previously was owned solely by Italians and European films.

1. Sophia Loren (standing) needs to be constantly pregnant to avoid jail time for the petty crime of selling contraband cigarettes to support her family, which puts the pressure on her not-very-ambitious husband Marcello Mastroianni (center).

2. The shallowness of Italy's idle rich is a subtle story point as Sophia Loren, whose husband is out of town on business, drives around Milan in a luxury Rolls Royce automobile while pondering an adulterous affair with her companion Marcello Mastroianni.

Actually, nobody even gets kissed in the 2 hours and 51 minutes of "My Fair Lady," but audiences haven't complained for decades. The 1964 musical film still entertains and has a pedigree of winning eight Oscars, including Best Picture.

Set in 1912 London, the movie examines events that transpire when an upper-class English gentleman portrayed by Rex Harrison, devotes himself to transforming a lowly young woman selling flowers in the street into a sophisticated lady.

That flower girl, Audrey Hepburn, speaks in the vowel-heavy Cockney accent of Britain's underclass, delivering such dialectic chestnuts as, "Aye wont to be a laadee," "move yer bloomin' arse," "koop ef taye" and "Ow, wats that eue saay?" Dressed in raggedly clothes and carrying on in a loutish manner, Hepburn is unrecognizable in the early stages of "My Fair Lady" as the sophisticated actress that audiences know.

Harrison and colleague Wilfrid Hyde-White play daffy upper class Englishmen consumed with remaking Hepburn. Through relentless linguistics drilling, Hepburn is transformed, though audiences expecting Hepburn and Harrison to fall in each other arms midway through "My Fair Lady" instead see Harrison revel in being a confirmed bachelor. "I prefer a new edition of Spanish inquisition / Than ever to let a woman in my life," he sings.

As Harrison brings Hepburn to high society events to test whether his student's newly-manufactured aristocratic accent fools London's upper crust, she catches the fancy of an earnest young man who becomes a suitor. Will Hepburn stay even though Harrison bullies her or go into the arms of the suitor?

"What I want is a little kindness," Hepburn tells Harrison in a climactic scene. "I know I'm a common ignorant girl...but I'm not dirt under your feet....I came to care for you not to want you to make love to me and not forgetting the difference between us. But more friendly like."

1964
My Fair Lady

Directed by GEORGE CUKOR

Starring: AUDREY HEPBURN (Eliza Doolittle) REX HARRISON (Professor Henry Higgins)
STANLEY HOLLOWAY / WILFRID HYDE-WHITE / GLADYS COOPER / JEREMY BRETT

Music by ALAN JAY LERNER / FREDERICK LOEWE

AUDREY HEPBURN, WHO USUALLY PLAYS ELEGANT CHARACTERS IN HER FILMS, IS BARELY RECOGNIZABLE AS YOUNG WOMAN SELLING FLOWERS IN THE STREETS OF EDWARDIAN ENGLAND, PRIOR TO HER BEING TRANSFORMED INTO A PROPER ENGLISH LADY.

1. Surprising herself a little, Audrey Hepburn enunciates proper English to the satisfaction of her tutors Wilfrid Hyde-White (left) and Rex Harrison, who transformed her from a slang-speaking street waif to a woman with upper-class polish.

2. London's wealthy class cheers the horses running at Ascot race track, where Audrey Hepburn (center of first row) momentarily forgets her recent crash course in manners and reverts to her working-class Cockney accent when she yells to a horse "move yer bloomin' arse!"

2 ▲

Such drama is leavened by dry humor throughout the film. When Hepburn accidently swallows one of several marbles in her mouth as part of a speech drill, Harrison seems unconcerned. "It doesn't matter," he says. "I've got 30 more. Open your mouth."

In another episode, Hepburn's conniving father shows up at Harrison's doorstep, angling for a five pound payment of hush money to keep silent about his daughter living in Harrison's big house. The father—played by Stanley Holloway—is told Harrison's intentions are honorable, to which he replies that if he thought Harrison had lecherous designs on his daughter "I'd ask for 50" pounds.

Holloway received an Oscar nomination for Best Supporting Actor, which is among "My Fair Lady's" whopping 12 Academy Award nominations. Its eight Oscar wins include Harrison for Best Actor and Hollywood legend George Cukor as Best Director, in addition to the coveted Best Picture victory. Except for a few ribald dialog-driven jokes, the movie's content is family-friendly.

1

The Warner Bros. Pictures' movie was a big box office hit and based on a smash Broadway stage play of the same name that was derived from the 1913 theater production "Pygmalion" by Irish playwright George Bernard Shaw. The movie takes place in Edwardian England, in an era where horse drawn carriages and early automobiles shared the streets of London.

The famous American song writing team of Alan Jay Lerner and Frederick Loewe created memorable music. Its most popular songs include "I Could Have Danced All Night," "With a Little Bit of Luck," "(I'm Getting Married in the Morning) Get Me to the Church On Time" and "I've Grown Accustomed to Her Face."

Hepburn's acting performance is considered top notch in "My Fair Lady," though she wasn't nominated for an Oscar in this role and Marni Nixon's singing was substituted in her musical performances. Interestingly, Hepburn was selected over Julie Andrews, who was paired opposite Harrison for the Broadway stage version, and Andrews won the Oscar for Best Actress that year for "Mary Poppins."

"Doctor Zhivago" is an epic romantic tragedy wrapped in an even larger tragedy. Omar Sharif—as Doctor Zhivago—spends a lifetime pursuing his true love, portrayed by Julie Christie. The backdrop of Russia's Bolshevik Revolution provides the larger tragedy of the violent remaking of Russian society with the slaughter of warfare and secret-police terror.

At its core, "Doctor Zhivago" is a tale of forbidden romance because Sharif and Christie are married to others. "Wouldn't it have been lovely if we'd met before?" the British-actress Christie wonders aloud. "We'd have gotten married, had a house and children." Sharif finds this thought of a happiness-that-might-have-been too painful to contemplate, saying, "I think we may go mad if we think about all that." Responds Christie, "I shall always think about it."

Sharif, who was Egyptian but passed for Russian with his chiseled good looks and a hairpiece of straight black hair covering his natural curls, fills the central role but is an uncomplicated, mostly-passive character who simply observes (except for some bursts of romantic passion). "We've been together six months on the road and here," Christie tells Sharif as he listens dewy-eyed and silent. "We've not done anything that you have to lie about to [your wife]. I don't want you to have to lie about me. You understand that?" After a pause, Christie sums up the Sharif character saying, "You understand everything."

The 1965 movie was based on the massive 600-page Boris Pasternak novel that was then unpublished in Russia because of its unflattering portrait of communism. The Metro-Goldwyn-Mayer release won five Oscars from 10 nominations, but lost to "The Sound of Music" for Best Picture.

The noteworthy supporting cast was led by Alec Guinness, who was a winner of two Oscars for other films and serves as the narrator of "Doctor Zhivago" in addition to being an on-screen character. The movie was his third collaboration with famed director David Lean following their "Lawrence of Arabia" and "Bridge on the River Kwai." The other well-known supporting actors were Geraldine Chaplin (daughter of silent film star Charlie Chaplin), Rod Steiger, Tom Courtenay and Ralph Richardson.

The movie was an immediate box-office hit, sparking fashion trends, men growing mustaches and a surge in naming babies Lara (Christie's character). But the film dates itself to the 1960s with female hairdos piled high in a dome effect with wavy bangs hanging to the sides—most conspicuously on Christie.

JULIE CHRISTIE (RIGHT) AND OMAR SHARIF (LEFT) ARE FORCED FROM THEIR COMFORTABLE LIVES IN MOSCOW TO RUSSIA'S HINTERLAND AND ITS BRUTAL WINTER IN THE SOCIETAL UPHEAVAL AFTER WORLD WAR I AND THE RUSSIAN REVOLUTION.

The movie's haunting signature music—referred to as "Lara's Theme" that became a hit song around the world—is a tearful serenade from the Russian three-string balalaika (prominent in the movie with its mandolin-like sound) that is made lusher with sorrowful orchestral strings and a deep male chorus. Composer Maurice Jarre won an Oscar for this musical score, which was later given lyrics as "Somewhere My Love".

When "Doctor Zhivago" premiered, critics were harsh, calling the epic an expensive soap opera. Some complained about gloomy framing of love scenes, even though they were intentionally shot dark to enhance the tragedy and be true to post-revolution squalor (the film won the Oscar for cinematography). Audiences immediately disagreed, propelling the $15 million production to a then-astronomical $200 million in global box offices.

In the aftermath of the Russian Revolution of 1917, a doctor, played by Omar Sharif returns to a vacation home that became an ice palace as it falls into disrepair. He writes poetry that becomes an underground sensation in Russia, though his prose is not appreciated by the Bolshevik regime.

«-Lara Antipova: Wouldn't it have been lovely if we'd met before?
-Doctor Yuri Zhivago: Before we did? Yes.-»

After beginning life in big-city prosperity, Julie Christie experiences years of hardship including working as a nurse in World War I and a lonely life in rural town afterwards, all the while buffeted by historical events in Russia and an elusive romance.

The most celebrated French-language film of the mid 1960s, "Un Homme et une Femme" ("A Man and a Woman") embodies the spirit of the era with its sometimes rough visual presentation, complicated narrative and sophisticated romance. "Un Homme et une Femme" is remembered for its very narrow story focus on two tortured, empty souls needing to be made whole and is credited for inspiring later films around the world with this same theme. In "Un Homme et Une Femme," all other characters are really merely props that move and say just a few lines.

The leading male character, portrayed by Jean-Louis Trintignant, meets the lovely Anouk Aimee at a boarding school, where the two young, single parents both have little children enrolled. While both are widowed, they are slow to reveal that they are unattached because of lingering pain from the untimely loss of their spouses. "You never talk about your wife," says Aimee, and this observation receives an uncomfortable silence.

"Un Homme et une Femme" does not present a particularly steamy romance, and is only moderately sexy by the standards of other French films that burst with obsession and lust. The romance does not become passionate until near the end of the film, and then Trintignant realizes his love is still mentally engaged with her deceased husband.

When they seemingly part company for the last time, Aimee simply says laconically, "I think I'd better take the train" instead of riding in Trintignant's car. But it is a false ending as their romance goes another chapter with a more satisfying conclusion.

The film has its quirks, though none are off-putting. Scenes alternate between black & white and color with no easily-discernable pattern, although flashback sequences are often in color. Many segments that are presented without dialog are covered by music or a character's voiceover.

1966
A Man and a Woman

Directed by CLAUDE LELOUCH

Starring: JEAN-LOUIS TRINTIGNANT (Jean-Louis Duroc)　ANOUK AIMÉE (Anne Gauthier)
PIERRE BAROUH / VALÉRIE LAGRANGE / ANTOINE SIRE

Music by FRANCIS LAI

Anouk Aimee and Jean-Louis Trintignant become acquainted because they have children who attend the same boarding school. He finds his new love Anouk Aimee has to work through hang-ups from tragedy in her life.

"Un Homme et Une Femme" is also noted for its frequent on-screen detours to scenes of professional auto races and street driving, because Trintignant's character is a professional race driver. The emphasis on vehicular action is very un-French, and a first-generation Ford Mustang that gets plenty of screen time seems out of place as an American-import pony car rumbling through the streets of Europe.

The one consistent criticism of the film is that the core love story is seemingly padded by car racing scenes. But the visuals of automotive action are stylish and engaging even for those with no interest in automobiles.

Claude Lelouch—the film's director, cinematographer and story creator—enjoyed a long career catapulted by "Un Homme et Une Femme" and its amazing haul of cinema awards. The movie won two Oscars in 1967—Best Foreign-Language Film and, in what was unusual for a non-Hollywood film, Best Original Screenplay. Lelouch's direction and Aimee's acting also received Oscar nominations. At the Cannes Film Festival, the romantic drama took the top prize and also won the Golden Globe as Best Foreign-Language Film, among its many accolades.

A free-spirited and amorous Jane Fonda struggles to loosen up her stiff and self-conscious husband portrayed by Robert Redford, and she steals most of their scenes in "Barefoot in the Park." The Fonda and Redford characters travel a bumpy road of mutual discovery as a newly-married couple, which makes for a sophisticated romantic comedy.

In a hotel hallway, Fonda embarrasses her new husband as they both exit an elevator full of strangers saying in a loud voice what would turn the head of any policeman, "Mr. Adams, I hope your realize that I'm only 15 years old." Redford is left to recoil, trying vainly trying to mute his horror to this humorous humiliation and a succession of other daffy episodes foisted on him by Fonda's uninhibited character.

"Barefoot in the Park" captures the daily indignities of living in impersonal and grimy New York City, starting with the newlywed's apartment, which is a run-down horror. Eccentric neighbors peek through doors open just a crack as Redford and Fonda pass, and stumble over empty cat food tins piled the hallway. French-born actor Charles Boyer shines in a secondary role as a mysterious elderly neighbor who flirts with newly-arrived Fonda after barging into her flat, apologizing when he finds it occupied and explaining that he needs to climb through her window to get into his apartment.

Redford and Fonda's journey of discovery is mostly amusing but not all laughs, as conflicts erupt from their vastly different personalities. "You are a funny kind of drunk, Paul," Fonda complains to Redford about being repressed at a restaurant. "You just sat around looking unhappy watching your coat (hanging on a coat rack)...That's no fun."

By the end of the movie, "Barefoot in the Park" is a case study that proves both the old Law of Physics and love...opposites attract. Redford suddenly becomes a free spirit, momentarily rattling Fonda. Over the course of the film, their love swings from suggestions that they are sex obsessed as newly married—which makes for several sight gags and witty dialog—to a more sophisticated love that audiences know is sustainable.

1967

Barefoot in the Park

Directed by GENE SAKS

Starring: ROBERT REDFORD (Paul Bratter)   JANE FONDA (Corie Bratter)
CHARLES BOYER / MILDRED NATWICK / HERBERT EDELMAN / MABEL ALBERTSON

Music by NEAL HEFTI

JANE FONDA PORTRAYS AN AFFECTIONATE AND WHIMSICAL NEWLY-WED WITH A PENCHANT FOR MISCHIEVOUS PRANKS AND PROVIDES A SHARP CONTRAST TO HER HUSBAND, ROBERT REDFORD, WHO IS A STUFFY NEW YORK LAWYER.

▲ 1

Knowing the rest of Redford's unconventional career—a charming con man in "The Sting," a succession of suave leading-man roles, an Oscar winner and guru of America's independent film movement—he seems slightly miscast as an emotionally-repressed office worker. Fonda amassed seven Oscar nominations and two Academy Award wins as a dramatic actress, and here she charms as an engaging sprite, though in this comedy role she was passed over by Oscar voters.

The funny dialog contains spot-on commentary about life in the big city and was penned by Neil Simon, who wrote the movie's screenplay based on his Broadway play. Simon's other notable works include "The Goodbye Girl," "The Odd Couple" with Jack Lemmon and "California Suite" again with Fonda.

The 1967 Paramount Pictures release also represents a bridge between the old Hollywood—evidenced by its musical score overflowing with syrupy violins—while introducing the strands of realism that would take Hollywood by storm by the 1970s. In various scenes, Fonda prances on screen wearing a revealing brassiere, brags about being "sexy," seriously suggests she wants a divorce and flops on a couch revealing her long, bare legs while giving a glimpse of the top of her stockings.

Today, this does not raise eyebrows. But those were all big no-nos in the formal code of old Hollywood that enforced a strict morality on-screen that was only gradually melting away when the film was released.

Since "Barefoot in the Park" is a comedy, the romance isn't passionate. What makes the film is its clever humor that is a sly commentary on ordinary life and marriage, and seeing two giants of cinema acting share the same screen just as they were entering true stardom.

2

1. Unleashing pent-up frustration, Robert Redford finally casts off his inhibitions by dancing barefoot in a New York City park. It's an unfamiliar characterization for audiences because Redford establishes himself as a suave leading man with his later films.

2. In a meeting of Oscar-winning lips, Robert Redford and Jane Fonda kiss while on a carriage ride in New York City's famous Central Park.

«-Ehtel Banks, (Corie's mother):
All you have to do is give up a little bit of you for him. Don't make everything a game, just late at night in that little room upstairs, take care of him. Make him feel...important. If you can do that, you'll have a happy and wonderful marriage, like one out of every ten couples. -»

"Bonnie and Clyde" is a classic film celebrated today for several reasons, any one of which alone would assure its place in cinema history. The 1967 film made up-and-comers Warren Beatty and Faye Dunaway into certified Hollywood screen stars. Its sympathetic treatment of a gang of notorious bank robbers is an early example of Hollywood then embracing cinema anti-heroes—referring to protagonists who lack admirable qualities—that came into fashion amid the social upheaval of the late 1960s. And the movie's graphic, bloody violence in gun-play scenes represents a sharp break from the sanitized action of earlier gangster films from major studios.

Dunaway (who portrays Bonnie) and Beatty (as gang leader Clyde Barrow) are two doomed lovers who nonchalantly embark on a life of crime, for which they gain fame. Besides portraying them as backwoods legends, the movie also shows them at times as pathetic. Beatty—who is presented as a handsome but low-life career criminal—is embarrassed by persistent sexual impotence and is terrified that he could get labeled as a homosexual. Dunaway—the sultry, gum-chewing waitress who joins Beatty to escape her dead-end life in Texas—later sums up their bleak existence from constantly running for their lives from the police, "You know what, when we started out, I thought we was really goin' somewhere. This is it?" Unable to express a complicated answer, Beatty awkwardly responds with just "I love you."

The two unlikely desperadoes are uneducated and poor from rural America, but the movie presents their love story as complex with tender, awkward and noble moments. When Dunaway briefly flees the safety of the gang because of pressures of constantly being on the run, Beatty character becomes genuinely distraught. After running down Bonnie in a corn field, Beatty pleads, "Please honey, don't ever leave me without saying nothing" as he hugs her in a teary, two-handed embrace. That line won't be confused with Shakespeare. But the fear of loss and the expression of passion by Beatty's character with those clumsy words are electric to Bonnie and cinema audiences.

The movie took some liberties with actual history, but is based on a true-life couple in the Great Depression of the 1930s. In real life and in the movie, the duo robs banks, roars out of towns in stolen cars, and captivates the public by sending photos of their exploits, poems and letters to newspapers. Newspapers gleefully print what they receive, turning the criminal duo into national celebrities. Their horrific end in a barrage of police bullets adds to their legend.

1967
Bonnie and Clyde

Directed by ARTHUR PENN

Starring: WARREN BEATTY (Clyde Barrow)   FAYE DUNAWAY (Bonnie Parker)
GENE HACKMAN / MICHAEL J. POLLARD / ESTELLE PARSONS / GENE WILDER

Music by CHARLES STROUSE

TWO LONELY LOSERS OF THE GREAT DEPRESSION, FAYE DUNAWAY AND WARREN BEATTY PURSUE A LIFE OF EXCITEMENT AND WEALTH WHILE DRIVING ACROSS COUNTRY TO ROB BANKS. THEIR 1930S CRIME SPREE MADE THE REAL-LIFE BONNIE AND CLYDE CULT HEROES TO SOME, AS THE POPULATION THAT WAS ANGRY ABOUT BANK FORECLOSURES OF HOMES WHOSE OWNERS WERE UNEMPLOYED.

The supporting cast is top notch including Gene Hackman, who portrays Beatty's brother and robbery partner, and comedian Gene Wilder, who spices up a serious role with dry humor when his character is briefly kidnapped by the gang.

Impressed by the gritty story, dramatic realism and watershed break with studio conventions, Hollywood showered the movie with 10 Oscar nominations. But the Warner Bros. Pictures release won Academy Awards in just two categories—supporting actress and cinematography.

Still, the film is a triumph for the vision of its two screenwriters and director Arthur Penn—who received Oscar nominations. Penn already was accomplished, with diverse credits in prestigious TV programs, theater and movies including the uplifting "The Miracle Worker." In "Bonnie and Clyde," Penn is remembered for his daring confidence in pushing violence and the anti-hero far beyond prevailing limits for mainstream Hollywood, instead of simply taking cautious half steps.

 While acclaimed today, "Bonnie and Clyde" was not an instant classic. When the movie was first released, its reception was shaky. Influential film critics wrote mixed or even harshly negative reviews complaining that the bloody crime spree was treated carelessly or even as absurd comedy. Interestingly, some of these same critics quickly reversed their appraisal, praising the realism embodied in "Bonnie and Clyde," that at its core depicts a desperate struggle by two outcasts of American society who share love in troubled times.

The dense prose of William Shakespeare never stirred romantic hearts as quite like it did with the 1968 movie "Romeo and Juliet," from director Franco Zeffirelli.

Its innovation was in casting young actors for the oft-told romantic drama about star-crossed lovers from enemy family clans in Italy. Critics marveled that they put more unbridled passion on the screen than older actors could have, given their preoccupation for measured and thoughtful performances of The Bard.

British actors Leonard Whiting and Olivia Hussey starred while they were in real life still teenagers. "Another year or two of (acting) experience, perhaps, and they would have been too intimidated to play the roles," wrote film critic Roger Ebert.

When the lovers seductively lock fingers and then embrace in an illicit rendezvous, Hussey—who portrays Juliet—de-

SNEAKING LIAISONS ON HER BALCONY, A YOUNG COUPLE—PORTRAYED BY BRITISH ACTORS OLIVIA HUSSEY AND LEONARD WHITING—ARE FROM WARRING CLANS IN TUDOR-ERA ITALY BUT IGNORE THEIR FAMILY FEUDS TO SECRETLY PURSUE THEIR PASSION. ▲

«-Juliet Capulet:
I shall stop loving you when I have finished counting the stars -»

Juliet stabs herself when she finds her Romeo lifeless in a tomb, after he took his own life when he mistakenly thought she was dead. It's a double tragic ending to the famous William Shakespeare play.

"Romeo and Juliet" is a European production fronted by British actors—Michael York is the best known among those in key supporting roles—and with Italians working in most of the behind-the-camera jobs. The English-language movie was filmed entirely in Italy.

The film won two Oscars for cinematography and costumes, and was also nominated in two other categories—both major—for Best Picture and Best Director for Zeffirelli. Many felt that "Romeo and Juliet" merited more recognition, but the dense Shakespearian dialog created a formal atmosphere that was a handicap with Academy Award voters. Further, the tragic ending of the lovers' demise creates a melodramatic flavor that may bring audiences to tears, but turns off serious-minded award voters.

"A glooming peace this morning with it brings," goes the famous closing narration. "The sun for sorrow will not show his head. For never was a story of more woe than this of Juliet and her Romeo." Famed Shakespearian actor Laurence Olivier is the film's narrator in an uncredited role.

In another handicap, when Paramount Pictures originally distributed the film, intense scenes were edited out to achieve a G general-audience rating for U. S. distribution. But a few years later, a more-appropriate to the subject matter PG-rated version was created that included some artful nudity.

The brightly-colored flowing costumes, men wearing tights as pants and both genders festooned in floppy hats give the film a rich period texture. Though this clothing represents Tudor-era Europe, it was also in step with the bold stripes and multicolored fashion of the 1960s. That fashion connection, along with the young cast, helped make the film relevant to teenagers. An even bigger attraction for the youth audience is the story's relevance about innocents suffering from the absurd feuds of their elders. That struck a chord in 1968 because of the Vietnam conflict and the Cold War, both then burning hot, and society was engulfed in political upheaval.

Hussey laments an artificial divide because of their warring families. "What's in a name?" she asks rhetorically from the balcony, in a signature line from the original Shakespeare play. "That which you call a rose by any other name would smell as sweet. So Romeo would ... without that title" of his family's name.

«-Romeo Montague:
Did my heart love till now? Forswear it, sight
For I never saw true beauty until this night.-»

"Love Story" represents a fascinating series of contradictions.

The 1970 tragic romance presents female lead Ali MacGraw offhandedly peppering her conversation with some salty words, which by then had became acceptable language in mainstream Hollywood films. Yet "Love Story" is a throwback as a tearjerker—meaning it is designed to make audiences cry—that piles on the old Hollywood clichés.

Signifying artistic praise, "Love Story" received seven Oscar nominations, including Best Picture. However, many critics dismissed movie as a formulaic contrivance. The contradictions continue because appreciative audiences made "Love Story" the top-grossing film of the year, attracted by its heavy-handed sentimentality.

"What can you say about a twenty-five-year-old girl who died?" heart-broken Ryan O'Neal says in an opening narration that is breathy and filled with emotional pauses. "That she was beautiful and brilliant. That she loved Mozart and Bach. The Beatles. And me."

O'Neal and MacGraw—who are both young, beautiful and energetic—meet while they are students at Harvard University and Radcliffe College, respectively. Those are among the prestigious schools clustered in the Northeast U.S. that churn out America's elite, so "Love Story" is also a window into the alluring world of privileged academia.

O'Neal is from a wealthy family while MacGraw is not. When they marry, there's disapproval from O'Neal's elitist father, who is portrayed by 1940s film star Ray Milland—winner of an acting Oscar in 1945.

While O'Neal is seen as emotional and hot-headed, MacGraw's character is more complex, confident and courageous as her end nears. "You are going to be the merry widower," MacGraw tells O'Neal. "I want you to be merry." After arguing, O'Neal finally gives in softly saying, "Okay," all the while being more emotional than MacGraw.

1970
Love Story

Directed by ARTHUR HILLER

Starring: RYAN O'NEAL (Oliver Barrett IV)   ALI MACGRAW (Jennifer Cavalleri)
JOHN MARLEY / RAY MILLAND

Music by FRANCIS LAI

AS FREE-SPIRITED NEWLY-WEDS AND WHILE DATING, RYAN O'NEAL AND ALI MACGRAW DASH AROUND THEIR COLLEGE TOWN IN O'NEAL'S BRITISH SPORTS CAR WHICH HE DRIVES WITH A TOUCH OF RECKLESSNESS.

1. and 2. After years of tension with his overbearing father, Ryan O'Neal breaks with his wealthy family to marry Ali MacGraw, who comes from a working-class background. Even though money is tight, the newly-weds are happy to simply have each other.

Love means never having to say you're sorry.

The film's most famous line of dialog is "Love means never having to say you're sorry," which most remember as delivered by MacGraw to O'Neal at a poignant moment.

But O'Neal also says the same words to Milland at the end of the film, which highlights their strained son-father relationship. (This relationship and O'Neal's life as a widower take center stage in a 1978 sequel movie that flopped, titled "Oliver's Story," whose title references the name of the O'Neal character.)

"Love Story" was based on a novel—which at the time was a giant best seller with more than 5 million copies sold—written by college professor and author Erich Segal. Segal, who taught classical literature at prestigious Yale University, also wrote the movie's screenplay.

But the credit for the movie's success is generally given to director Arthur Hiller, who has a string of studio film credits. Hiller provided color and back-story that made the two lead characters likeable to audiences. When released, the 1 hour, 39 minute film received a slightly-restrictive PG rating for fleeting rough language and brief bedroom scenes.

"Love Story's" only Oscar win came for Best Original Music Score by French composer Francis Lai, whose simple piano melody is both haunting and romantic. Hiller, Segal, MacGraw and O'Neal received Oscar nominations.

The film is also noteworthy for providing a young Tommy Lee Jones (who in a real life had been a student at Harvard) with his first role in a major film, though it's just a cameo as one of O'Neal's card-playing college chums.

As for knocks, critics complain that the MacGraw-O'Neal relationship is just too perfect and predictable. And they contend that once MacGraw is diagnosed with a fatal disease two-thirds of the way through the film, performances by the two lead actors lack depth and nuance.

But audiences didn't necessarily agree. "Love Story," along with "The Godfather" and "Rosemary's Baby" helped revive Paramount Pictures from near death after suffering from a string of flops.

Throughout the history of cinema romance, opposites on the screen are attracted to each other and this notion is central to the unlikely love story driving "The Way We Were."

In the 1973 romantic drama, Barbra Streisand portrays a headstrong leftist political activist, whose marriage to easygoing pragmatist Robert Redford is buffeted by the currents of U.S. history from the mid-1930s to the 1950s. Their romance presents a sharp on-screen contrast between the demonstrative Streisand and the cool and steady Redford.

"You have no sense of humor," Redford complains to Streisand when they meet in college, circa class of 1937. "Why are you always so angry?"

Streisand denies being "always" strident. She then mischievously uses Redford's sunny disposition to put him on the defensive. "Can I ask you a personal question?" Streisand retorts. "(Why) do you smile all the time?"

They're also contrasts in that she's frizzy-haired and Jewish while he's a handsome blond WASP.

"You'll never find anyone as good for you as I am, to believe in you as much as I do or to love you as much," she tells him in an emotional moment. The level-headed Redford replies without fanfare, "I know that."

Redford is attracted to Streisand because of her moxie and her intellect, and he relies on her smarts when they move to Hollywood, where he becomes a writer and she pursues a career in the media business. In constant banter at home, they discuss stories and ideas that, on one occasion, Streisand uses to reveal she's with child.

"I've got one for you," she says, as if discussing just another random story idea. "Loudmouth Jewish girl from New York City comes to Malibu, California and tells her gorgeous 'goyish' guy that she's pregnant, you see. And he, just, looks at her and..." Streisand says as her voice trails off. Realizing this isn't just another made-up story, Redford twists his head to see Streisand beaming with a smile of satisfaction.

1973
The Way We Were

Directed by SYDNEY POLLACK

Starring: ROBERT REDFORD (Hubbel Gardiner) **BARBRA STREISAND** (Katy Morosky)
BRADFORD DILLMAN / LOIS CHILES / PATRICK O'NEAL

Music by MARVIN HAMLISCH

A CHANCE MEETING AT A NIGHT CLUB DURING WORLD WAR II REKINDLES AN OLD FRIENDSHIP FROM COLLEGE THAT EVENTUALLY MORPHS INTO A ROMANCE. BARBRA STREISAND WORKS AT A RADIO STATION AND SPOTS ROBERT REDFORD, WHO IS A U.S. NAVAL OFFICER.

"Annie Hall" is a sophisticated romantic comedy that at first glance resembles the low-brow comedies that were filmmaker Woody Allen's hallmark until this 1977 masterpiece—which won the Oscar for Best Picture. It's loaded with non-stop absurdist humor, characters talking to the camera (directly addressing the audience), split screens, and Allen kvetching about his numerous neuroses.

Among the memorably-unconventional scenes, Allen—who is the director, co-writer and leading man—and Diane Keaton strain to be intellectual while conversing over drinks, while subtitles reveal their real thoughts. "I wonder what she looks like naked?" flashes one subtitle of what's actually on Allen's mind.

That's typical of the goofiness up to that point in Allen's career, with sophomoric comedy films like "Bananas" and "Sleeper" that essentially string together sketch humor. "Annie Hall" represents a pivotal transition to authentic characters in increasingly realistic stories, and started Allen on his path for 21 Oscar nominations.

Besides launching Allen as a serious filmmaker, "Annie Hall" won four Oscars in major categories—Best Picture, Best Actress for Keaton, and Best Director and Best Original Screenplay for Allen. In addition, Allen was nominated as Best Actor.

In the PG-rated film distributed by United Artists, Allen provides keen insights about relationships, society and one's personal outlook on life. "Hey listen, give me a kiss," the nerdy and perpetually-anxious Allen tells Keaton as they walk down the street when first meeting. "We never kissed before...And, and there will be that tension, you know."

In this perceptive comment that audiences know worries guys everywhere on first dates, Allen continues, "I'll never know when to make the right move or anything. So we'll kiss now, get it over with and then we'll go eat."

Then for an Allen-esque exclamation point to the scene, he rationalizes his notion saying with dry humor, "We'll digest our food better." They do a short kiss and then quickly head for a restaurant.

1977
Annie Hall

Directed by WOODY ALLEN

Starring: DIANE KEATON (Annie Hall)   WOODY ALLEN (Alvy Singer)
TONY ROBERTS / CAROL KANE / PAUL SIMON / CHRISTOPHER WALKEN / JEFF GOLDBLUM / SIGOURNEY WEAVER

DIANE KEATON'S BAGGY MEN'S CLOTHING BECAME A FASHION RAGE IN THE 1970S. HERE, SHE CONVERSES CLUMSILY WITH WHITE-CLAD WOODY ALLEN ON A NEW YORK CITY ROOFTOP.

There's also a steady stream of Allen's trademark comedy of the absurd, much of which comes off as a cultural insights intended for movie-industry insiders. From Allen's New York City-centric viewpoint, the film constantly bashes Los Angeles and the omnipresent Hollywood, though the knocks are really clichés. When at a Hollywood party, Allen overhears another guest in this bit of Hollywood-babble: "Right now it's only a notion, but I think I get money, make it into a concept and then later turn it into an idea."

New York culture takes a few gentle knocks as well. Informed that two college professors holding prestigious chairs are in the same room with him, Allen is unimpressed, saying, "Two more chairs and they've got a dining room set."

Keaton's baggy boy's wardrobe also caught the eye of the female audience, sparking a fashion trend of women wearing oversized, male-like suit jackets, pants and very wide ties. Keaton's character grows up from an undemanding sprite in the big city (carefree in saying "La-di-da, la-di-da, la la") to someone with serious aspirations in love and career.

▲ 1

She outgrows the relationship with the little-changed Allen, after he encourages her to become more self-reliant. "Yeah, well you wanted to keep the relationship 'flexible,'" she shoots back at Allen in one scene. "Remember, it's your phrase?"

Another element that elevates the film is its excellent supporting cast. Secondary roles are filled by Tony Roberts, Carol Kane, singer/actor Paul Simon, Shelley Duvall, Colleen Dewhurst and Christopher Walken. In addition, two soon-to-be-famous actors fill very minor roles that helped launch their careers: Jeff Goldblum (whose only line, "I forgot my mantra" is delivered in passing at a Hollywood party) and Sigourney Weaver.

"Annie Hall" was originally conceived as a lengthy murder mystery, but a large murder sub-plot was dropped and the final movie runs 1 hour, 34 minutes. The eliminated storyline inspired Allen's "Manhattan Murder Mystery" years later that also stars Keaton.

...You know how you're always trying to get things to come out perfect in art ... because it's so difficult in life.

1. Diane Keaton is a farm girl from Middle America finding her way into a career in the big city where Woody Allen already has an established career and prestige. Once she establishes herself, they drift apart.

2. They're both a little neurotic and, while attracted to each other, it's still awkward as Woody Allen and Diane Keaton kiss while sitting on a couch.

"On Golden Pond" is a bittersweet look at the end of a lifelong love affair. Elderly characters portrayed by Henry Fonda—a crotchety 80-year-old—and his even-keeled wife Katharine Hepburn are sustained by sweet memories of a lifetime together.

"We're not middle aged," jokes Fonda with mock seriousness to Hepburn. "You're old and I'm ancient."

Behind the geriatric jokes, Fonda is losing his mental faculties—and he and Hepburn know it. This makes for poignant moments and lots of hugging as they cope. "I came running back here to you and your pretty face," an emotional Fonda admits after getting lost on a simple excursion. "I could feel safe."

Every scene takes place around a scenic New England summer home on the shores of a small lake known as Golden Pond. But audiences mostly don't notice the confined setting, because the natural beauty of the shoreline, stretches of blue water and lush woods project a sense of vastness on the cinema screen.

There's a parallel story line about a torn father-daughter relationship between Henry and Jane Fonda—a father-daughter team as movie characters and in real life. When the younger Fonda complains about father to her screen mother Hepburn, to whom she is close, Hepburn responds, "Here we go again." Then Hepburn delivers this dose of tough love while embracing her daughter. "You had a miserable childhood, your father was overbearing and your mother ignored you...Don't you think that everyone looks back on their childhood with a certain amount of bitterness and regrets about something? It doesn't have to ruin your life, darling."

The 1981 film, distributed by Universal Pictures won four Oscars out of 10 nominations, though Best Picture went to Olympics drama "Chariots of Fire." Hepburn—who gets first billing—and Henry Fonda received two of those Oscars in their respective acting categories, and Ernest Thompson won another for the screenplay adaptation of his own stage play.

1981
On Golden Pond

Directed by MARK RYDELL

Starring: KATHARINE HEPBURN (Ethel Thayer) HENRY FONDA (Norman Thayer Jr.)
JANE FONDA / DOUG MCKEON / DABNEY COLEMAN

Music by DAVE GRUSIN

LONGTIME A MARRIED COUPLE, KATHARINE HEPBURN AND HENRY FONDA SUMMER AT GOLDEN POND EVERY YEAR. THIS TIME IN PARTICULAR THEY TAKE STOCK OF LIFE AND THEIR LIVES AS FONDA'S FAILING HEALTH IS A LOOMING CRISIS.

For the elder Fonda, it was the only Best Actor Oscar win in his distinguished career. The role can be viewed as a gift from daughter Jane, who originally optioned the film rights to the stage play (she received an Oscar nomination for her supporting role). The Best Actress Oscar was Hepburn's career-capping fourth Academy Award out of 12 nominations.

The movie's most memorable scene serves up uncomfortable humor when the elder Fonda's curmudgeon character listens as his grown daughter's new boyfriend—played by character actor Dabney Coleman—asks if can share a bedroom with the daughter while visiting.

At first, Fonda pretends to think that Coleman wants three persons in the same bed. Then the straight-faced Fonda lowers the boom saying, "I guess I'd be delighted to have you *abuse* my daughter under my own roof. Would you like the room where I first violated her mother?"

That memorable scene shows that "On Golden Pond" isn't all tears, hugs and reminiscing. Touches of humor helped it become the second-highest grossing film of 1981, which is an achievement for what is essentially a sentimental slice of life about two old people.

158-159 Katharine Hepburn and Henry Fonda both won the Oscars for their acting performances that are funny, poignant and sad, in this story about the struggle to heal old family wounds.

A U.S. Naval base on the Pacific Coast is an intense hot-house, as young officers train to be military pilots by day, and romance local women by night in "An Officer and a Gentleman." Everyone, including a local woman portrayed by Debra Winger who has a fling with Navy cadet Richard Gere, knows the military men are just passing through on the road to bright careers.

They hit it off well at a dance. But then Gere becomes withdrawn after he is forced into a short street fight in which he beats up a young local man who is angry that military men are dating local women. "You know, Zack (Gere's character), it wouldn't kill you to open up to me a little bit," Winger says with her voice quivering when they are alone in a motel room afterwards. "I'm trying to be nice to you," she continues. "I'm trying to be your friend, Zack."

Refusing to open up, Gere coldly replies, "Well then, be a friend. Get out of here."

"An Officer and a Gentleman"—a 1982 release—gradually reveals that both lovers are wounded people. Each experienced wrenching abandonment as children, making them sympathetic to the audience, who roots for their relationship to blossom.

Gere was raised by a heartless, heavy-drinking father who is a Navy enlisted man—played by Oscar-winner Robert Loggia in a supporting role. Winger, who works at a paper factory, is one of the pretty faces at military dances whom the military men privately sneer at as just trashy locals.

Later, when Gere starts to tell Winger frankly that he sees their relationship as only sexual, she cuts him off, saying, "I know who you are and what you want." Winger then professes no interest in a permanent relationship. "That's it?" Gere asks, surprised and attracted by her spunky independence.

Gere's friend from training, portrayed by David Keith, has a parallel romance with Winger's friend played by Lisa Blount, which gets even more tangled as the 2 hour, 4 minute movie progresses. The two romances present a stark contrast of a manipulative love versus one that is honest but risks everything.

In most romance movies, the subplots tend to be in the background, but this story is substantial in "An Officer and a Gentleman." Gere's road to personal redemption is to finish the rigorous training to be a Navy flyer.

Louis Gossett Jr. portrays the relentless Navy training instructor pushing his recruits to the limit of physical endurance in order to identify those who don't have the right stuff to be aviators. His coarse language includes crude personal insults and repellant comments about the damage warplanes might cause innocent civilians.

1982
An Officer and a Gentleman

Directed by TAYLOR HACKFORD

Starring: RICHARD GERE (Zack Mayo)   DEBRA WINGER (Paula Pokrifki)
DAVID KEITH / ROBERT LOGGIA / LISA BLOUNT

Music by JACK NITZSCHE

WHEN NEWLY-COMMISSIONED U.S. NAVY OFFICER RICHARD GERE DECIDES TO MARRY WORKING-CLASS LOCAL WOMAN DEBRA WINGER, HE LETS EVERYONE KNOW AT WINGER'S FACTORY JOB BY LITERALLY CARRYING HER OFF TO A NEW LIFE.

Such rough language, brief sex scenes and one gruesome death result in "An Officer and A Gentleman" getting a well-deserved R-rating, even though the movie is ultimately uplifting.

In a memorable scene when Gossett threatens to boot Gere out of the Navy, an exhausted Gere shouts pathetically, "Don't you do it! Don't! You... I got nowhere else to go! I got nowhere else to ggg...," Gere's sobbing voice then trails off. "I got nothin' else."

Gossett won the Oscar for Best Supporting Actor as the hard-driving drill sergeant in a nuanced performance. "An Officer and a Gentleman" also won a second Oscar for Best Original Song. The Paramount Pictures release also received four other Academy Award nominations, including for Winger as Lead Actress.

This role was one reason that Debra Winger's career soared in the 1980s and into the early 1990s. Gere has emerged as a bigger star with a longer run on the top, though he doesn't have any Oscar kudos to his credit.

"An Officer and a Gentleman's" signature scene presents Gere—dressed in an impressive Navy uniform of white from hat-to-shoes—arriving unannounced at Winger's paper factory job. He literally sweeps her off her feet by carrying her out to the applause of her many co-workers, who are more accustomed to Navy officers that love-and-then-leave them.

A surprisingly frank plea by Meryl Streep to her future husband demonstrates the fierce independent streak of her character and why the script of "Out of Africa" won an Oscar for Best Adapted Screenplay.

"You could marry me," Streep tells friend Klaus Maria Brandauer. He tries to put her off, replying with a laugh, "I have to marry a virgin. I can't stand criticism."

Streep, who covets the title baroness that such a union would give her, continues undeterred, "For the money, I mean...listen to me. I have no life at all. And now I failed to marry. You know the punishment for that. And you have gone through all your money. You're off seducing the servant girls. We're a pair you and I. At least we're friends. We might be all right."

Streep is an unhappy upper-class woman in pre-World War I Denmark, which she soon escapes to start farm in Africa, marry likeable scoundrel Brandauer and romance a macho big game hunter played by Robert Redford. The 1985 epic romance "Out of Africa" won seven Oscars, including Best Picture.

Arriving in British East Africa in 1913 for farming, Streep becomes attached to Africa and native Africans, while just barely getting along with fellow white settlers—mostly British—who are callous toward the black population. Setting up a romance between two Oscar winners who are giants of cinema, Streep gravitates to Redford who is American. "If you say anything now," a breathy Streep tells him in their first passionate liaison while in a tent on a safari. "I'll believe it."

While Steep's husband Brandauer has faded from her life, Redford is not the type to make a commitment and is frequently gone on business, refusing to be a grounded farmer. "Why is your freedom more important than mine?" Streep complains to Redford in a lovers' quarrel, saying her needs aren't being met. "You don't need me," counters Redford, pointing out that if he died she'd keep on living. "You always confuse need with want."

1985
Out of Africa

Directed by SYDNEY POLLACK

Starring: MERYL STREEP (Karen Blixen) ROBERT REDFORD (Denys Finch-Hatton)
KLAUS MARIA BRANDAUER

Music by JOHN BARRY

EXHAUSTED UPON RETURN FROM A TRIP IN THE AFRICAN BUSH, ROBERT REDFORD FALLS ASLEEP ON MERYL STREEP'S FARMHOUSE PORCH. WHEN STREEP LATER COMPLAINS HE'S ALWAYS LEAVING, THE INDEPENDENT-MINDED REDFORD REPLIES, "I DO COME BACK. ALL THE TIME."

▲ 1

«- ... Perhaps he knew, as I did not, that the Earth was made round so that we would not see too far down the road.-»

Redford's character is so withdrawn and aloof that some film critics say the romance suffers because there's no bonfire-like passion. As a character detached from colonial society, Redford frets that the wild Africa he loves is being lost to creeping Western-style development in the 1920s and 1930s. Most of "Out of Africa" was filmed in Kenya, capturing the magnificent colors, fauna and wildlife. Northern England doubled for a few shots of Denmark.

While the romance story pursues a trajectory of tragedy, "Out of Africa" is entertaining with some humor. When Redford lands a newly-acquired bi-plane, he picks up Streep to give her an aerial view of Africa. "When did you learn to fly?" asks an incredulous Streep as she boards his plane. "Yesterday," answers Redford as he suppresses a grin.

"Out of Africa" from Universal Pictures received 11 Academy Award nominations for 1985, winning seven. Besides Best Picture, Sydney Pollack—who directed Redford in the Western drama "Jeremiah Johnson" in 1972—won in the major category of Best Director. Streep and Austria-born Brandauer were Oscar-nominated as actors.

1. Klaus Maria Brandauer looks the part of a roguish European settler in early 1900s Africa, as he decked out in a safari outfit and surrounded by native Africans.

2. Meryl Streep and her on-screen husband Klaus Maria Brandauer are by all appearances a respectable married couple who are European settlers in Africa. But his philandering wrecks their marriage, although they remain friends.

1. Meryl Streep portrays a self-reliant Danish woman who flees the comforts and restrictions of European high society to start a farm in a remote part of colonial British East Africa in 1913, falling in love with Africa and some of the men around her.

2. Robert Redford portrays an aloof American who hunts and leads safaris in Africa in the early 1900s. When World War I breaks out, he doesn't want to take sides and when lover Meryl Streep wants a commitment, he asks "how would a wedding change things" for the better.

▲ 1

With a slightly restricted PG-rated audience classification, the epic runs 2 hours, 41 minutes and is loosely based on the real life of Karen Blixen, a Danish-born woman wrote about her African experiences under the pen name Isak Dinesen.

In a sly screen reference to the movie's source, Redford gives Streep (who portrays Blixen) a fancy pen as a gift for her entertaining and elaborate story-telling at dinner. "But my stories are free," protests Streep who doesn't immediately accept the expensive pen. "Write them down sometime," Redford replies.

Though cleaning up in awards, "Out of Africa" was the fifth ranked film at U.S. box office in 1985. The top-ranked was the whimsical comedy "Back to the Future" which generated 140% more in box office revenue while costing an estimated 40% less to produce.

«-Denys (Redford): You've ruined it for me, you know.
-Karen Blixen (Streep): Ruined what?
-Denys (Redford): Being alone.-»

1. Meryl Streep and Robert Redford are in the upper echelons of colonial society in 1913 British East Africa, but both are misfits. They are more comfortable with untamed Africa and, over time, with each other.

2. Redford coaxes Meryl Streep to tour the remote beauties of Africa before colonial expansion changes the countryside. At a stop to camp for the night, he washes her hair.

Helena Bonham Carter plays Beethoven on a piano with intense passion, but lives an emotionally repressed life of the upper class that is characteristic of 1908 England. In "A Room with a View," her character gets engaged to be married to self-absorbed intellectual portrayed by Daniel Day-Lewis, but two chance kisses of electric passion with another man tear her heart.

The 1985 movie came from Merchant Ivory Productions, which stood as a sort of brand-name for intellectually-dense but nonetheless engaging period dramas in its heyday of the 1980s and 1990s. Its credits include the also-acclaimed "Howards End" and "The Remains of the Day."

In a hallmark of the complex and layered storytelling of Merchant Ivory, the romantic story in "A Room with a View" is advanced and illuminated by secondary characters and not just the lovers themselves. "My poor boy has brains, but he's very muddled," an elderly father Denholm Elliott pleads to Carter in a personal moment. "I don't require you to fall in love with my boy, but please try to help him. If anyone can stop him from brooding."

That muddled son is the handsome but disconnected-from-society Julian Sands, whose character later twice grabs Carter—the pouty-faced and bushy-haired beauty—for spontaneous passionate kisses. He makes no explanation, which is unusual for cinema romance, and Carter visibly recoils from the breaches of Edwardian-society etiquette. But movie-goers wonder if her soul is secretly stirred.

"You don't mean you are going to marry that man?" Sands finally opens up in a climactic scene near the end of the film, upon learning Carter is engaged to the aloof Day-Lewis. "He wants you for a possession—something to look at like a painting or ivory box. He doesn't want you to be real and to think and to live. He doesn't love you. But I love you. I want to you to have your own thoughts and ideas and feelings even when I hold you in my arms."

Carter is left to choose between passion and societal convention. When she soon breaks up with Day-Lewis, Carter awkwardly parrots Sands' speech to explain, which leaves Day-Lewis bewildered on screen but amuses audiences to no end since they know the source of her labored words. Clever, dry humor often breaks the monotony of the serious dramas that made Merchant Ivory films such hits. And there's a lesser dash of farcical humor, such as ladies strolling in the woods who come across three male characters, skinny dipping in a pond to escape the summer heat, as was the custom at the time.

1985

A Room with a View

Directed by JAMES IVORY

Starring: HELENA BONHAM CARTER (Lucy Honeychurch)   JULIAN SANDS (George Emerson)
DANIEL DAY-LEWIS / MAGGIE SMITH / JUDI DENCH / DENHOLM ELLIOTT / PATRICK GODFREY / RUPERT GRAVES

A BROODING CHARACTER PORTRAYED BY JULIAN SANDS SHOCKS THE RESERVED HELENA BONHAM CARTER WITH AN IMPULSIVE KISS WHEN THEY ARE ALONE ON A TOURIST OUTING IN ITALY. SUCH FAMILIARITY IS STRICTLY FORBIDDEN BY EUROPEAN CULTURE IN THE EARLY 1900S, BUT CARTER DOESN'T RESIST TOO MUCH.

«-Mr. Emerson:
There's only one thing impossible.
That's to love and to part.-»

1 ▲
2 ▶

Filmed at a modest cost of $3 million that is less than one fifth of a Hollywood major studio movie at the time (despite the expensive Edwardian period costumes), "A Room with a View" is an inexpensive film that made Oscar headlines with three Academy Awards and another five nominations, including Best Picture. Its only major category Oscar win was for Best Adapted Screenplay by Ruth Prawer Jhabvala—a two-time Oscar winner and frequent collaborator with James Ivory (who was nominated for Best Director) and producer Ismail Merchant.

Besides its romance, the film is acclaimed as a faithful screen adaptation of the novel by E. M. Forester that delivered a cutting commentary on cultural repression in British high society prior to World War I. The title comes from characters discussing the panoramas visible from their hotel windows—or a lack of such vistas—while visiting Italy, where they meet by chance and they later reunite in England.

The movie sports an all-star British cast that includes Carter, Maggie Smith, Elliott, Sands, Simon Callow, Judi Dench, Day-Lewis and Rupert Graves. Day-Lewis—whose father was a poet laureate of Britain—and Smith are two-time Oscar winners, and Dench received one Oscar—all for other movies.

1. Helena Bonham Carter looks the part of an elegant and privileged woman who conforms to the strict rules of social behavior in England's Edwardian era of the early 1900s.

2. As a young woman coming of age, Helena Bonham Carter (seated at center) struggles to decide which of two completely-different male suitors she really loves; her family and the code of conduct for English high-society force her to suppress her true emotions.

In 13th Century Italy, an evil ruler and a sorcerer's spell stand between two lovers who are separated by a curse. This is the supernatural medieval world of "Ladyhawke," which is a bouncy movie with castles, sword fights and dungeons that occasionally rocks to a soundtrack of throbbing techno-pop music.

"I have not seen what I have just seen," Matthew Broderick says speaking to the heavens after seeing a pretty woman inexplicably calm a wild wolf in the woods. "These are magical, unexplainable matters. And I beg you not to make me part of them."

Alas, Broderick's wish is not granted because the 1985 movie is told from his ever-deeper involvement. The impish-faced young actor portrays a likeable scalawag who escapes a dank dungeon to help Michelle Pfeiffer and Rutger Hauer—the star crossed lovers. "Ladyhawke" presents their characters' story in a romantic drama with a lot of fantasy and touch of comedy.

The story is also a mystery that unfolds slowly. "There was a woman like fine porcelain with deep blue eyes," Broderick tells warrior Hauer of an encounter in the woods. "Almost like a bird's. And her voice that does fit the dulcet tones of an angel... I asked her if I was dreaming and she said I was."

The story is based on a centuries-old, fanciful story about two lovers "always together, eternally apart" who are separated by the curse.

Hauer roams the countryside—dressed in black but a good guy at heart—accompanied by a bird from which the film draws its title. It's not exactly clear why the hawk is so dear to him and he talks to the bird like it is human, saying in a trembling voice, "Don't be afraid" when the hawk is injured.

Pfeiffer is also cryptic. When Broderick asks Pfeiffer whether she is "flesh or spirit," the pretty blonde answers softly, "I am sorrow" but does not elaborate.

"Ladyhawke" presents a brief graphic scene of executions and plenty of sword-fighting, which earns it a mildly restrictive PG-13 audience classification in the USA, along with its occasional bawdy humor.

1985
Ladyhawke

Directed by RICHARD DONNER

Starring: MICHELLE PFEIFFER (Isabeau D'Anjou) RUTGER HAUER (Etienne Navarre)
MATTHEW BRODERICK / LEO MCKERN / JOHN WOOD /

Music by ANDREW POWELL

A RARE CELESTIAL OCCURRENCE GIVES MICHELLE PFEIFFER AND HER LOVE RUTGER HAUER THE OPPORTUNITY TO SHATTER THE CURSE THAT HAS KEPT THEM APART, REWARDING THEIR COURAGE AFTER THEY TAKE CONSIDERABLE RISKS.

At one point, the cowardly street brat Broderick refuses a heroic assignment, saying, "Not for the life of my mother! Even if I knew who she was." Another mature element is a subtle anti-church undercurrent because a nasty bishop is the film's bad guy.

The cast is a mix of Europeans—among them the Dutch Hauer—and Americans Broderick and Pfeiffer. "Ladyhawke" did not get Academy Award nods in any major categories, though in later movies Pfeiffer would receive three Oscar nominations for acting. However, "Ladyhawke" was nominated for two Oscars in technical categories. The 2 hour long movie is a joint effort of major studios Warner Bros. and 20th Century Fox.

The supporting cast, which is mostly from the United Kingdom, gets some choice lines and screen time. The evil bishop, portrayed by British actor John Wood, exudes sinister coolness as the tormentor who drives the wedge that separates the two lovers. "Great storms announce themselves as a simple breeze, captain," he tells a henchmen when given bad news. "And a single random spark can ignite the fires of rebellion."

Rutger Hauer provides a perch for the film's namesake Ladyhawke as they roam Medieval Italy. It's not immediately clear what they seek but some strange magic is in the air. ◄

In an inchanted 13th Century Medieval world, Michelle Pfeiffer's sorrowful character suffers under a curse that means that she is "always together, eternally apart" from her love. ▶

Great storms announce themselves with a single breeze.

The director Richard Donner—an American—was emerging as an A-list Hollywood talent when "Ladyhawke" was made, and has a knack for delivering bouncy, popular movies. His career credits include the original 1978 "Superman" and the four action-adventure "Lethal Weapon" movies.

In theatrical release, "Ladyhawke" was not a blockbuster, though it later became a TV and DVD favorite. Some were cool to the film's brash humor and a number of the movie's scenes are presented in annoyingly low light, although they are contrasted by quick transitions to sunshine morning scenes, which are a bit of a jolt.

Still, "Ladyhawke" is impressive with scenes filmed at authentic Italian castles that are charming in their crumbling glory, and there's plenty of swashbuckling adventure as the drama unfolds.

Hollywood has a long-running fascination with Italian Americans in New York City ranging from "The Godfather" to "Saturday Night Fever" to "Raging Bull." "Moonstruck" returns to this familiar turf but its real epicenter is the kitchen table, where vast quantities of food get eaten and often-volcanic life unfolds for Italian-American families.

When Cher—who portrays a 37 year-old widow—tells her father that she's getting re-married, they are sitting—where else—at the kitchen table of the family home in the borough of Brooklyn. "Again?" responds father played by jowl-faced Vincent Gardenia. "You did this once before and it didn't work out...don't get married again, Loretta" (Cher's character).

Cher's mother, played by Olympia Dukakis, doesn't show any more enthusiasm moments later, though she's pleased when Cher says she's not deeply in love with her fiancé. "Good," replies the gray-haired Dukakis, drawing on the wisdom of her years. "When you love them, they drive you crazy because they know they can." (Cher defends her choice saying her fiancé played by Danny Aiello is a "sweet man").

"Moonstruck" is a 1987 romantic comedy with a touch of the supernatural. The film's title references excesses of the heart that mysteriously erupt when an unusually bright and large moon shines on Brooklyn. In one such a moon-washed period, the 1 hour, 42 minute film squeezes in several parallel romances, ranging from love triangles to a sordid extra-marital affair to the happily married . The marital cheating, some brief rough language and very brief bedroom scenes contribute to a mildly-restrictive PG rating.

To flesh out the crazy-quilt of love stories, director Norman Jewison put together an ensemble cast of mostly character actors—familiar faces known to audiences for filling a narrow type of supporting role. Many of those characters are Cher's family, living together in a roomy home and constantly chattering around the kitchen table.

Atop that cast are stars Cher and Nicolas Cage, who portrays the estranged brother of Aiello. Cage's character is emotional with pent up rage, yet Cher finds herself attracted to Cage, who alternately acts like a maniac and then later is soothed by the soaring music of Italian opera.

1987
Moonstruck

Directed by NORMAN JEWISON

Starring: CHER (Loretta Castorini)   NICOLAS CAGE (Ronny Cammareri)
OLYMPIA DUKAKIS / VINCENT GARDENIA / DANNY AIELLO / JULIE BOVASSO / JOHN MAHONEY

Music by DICK HYMAN

"You're gonna marry my brother?" Cage says as he walks down the street alone with Cher. "Why you wanna sell your life short? Playing it safe is just about the most dangerous thing a woman like you could do... why didn't you wait for the right man?"

Cher shoots back, "Because he didn't come" to which Cage answers, "I'm here!" Then Cher pauses to look at Cage squarely in the eye with her big flowing hair completely framing the top and sides of her face. "You're late," she says.

At another juncture, Cage blames Cher for running his life. "That's impossible," Cher shouts back. "It was ruined when I got here."

"Moonstruck" won three Academy Awards including two for acting—Cher as Best Lead Actress and Dukakis as Best Supporting Actress. The Metro-Goldwyn-Mayer release was also nominated in three other categories, including Best Picture and Best Director for Jewison, who has multiple directing and producing Academy Award nominations.

The film's third Oscar win was in Best Original Screenplay for John Patrick Shanley, who was then mostly known for edgy off-Broadway stage plays. Growing up Irish Catholic in New York, he was envious of his Italian neighbors who were more emotionally demonstrative amid a perpetual chaos that oddly never got completely out of hand. This chaos is at the heart of "Moonstruck."

Shanley's dialog for Cage captures the heat of romantic emotions that churn throughout the movie. "Love don't make things nice," Cage tells Cher. "It ruins everything. It breaks your heart. It makes things a mess."

▲ 1

▲ 2

1. and 2. Nicolas Cage portrays the estranged brother of Cher's fiancée when they meet and are immediately attracted to each other. Though he played the role of a 30-something man, match the age of Cher's character, Cage was actually at age 23—15 years younger than Cher—when "Moonstruck" was released.

The male-female relationship in modern society is portrayed as relentless numbing warfare in romantic comedy "When Harry Met Sally..." because neither gender really comprehends the nuances of the other. A relationship between Billy Crystal, who portrays the breezy and uninhibited Harry, and Meg Ryan, who is the fussy and emotional Sally, starts off as mutual disdain and then morphs into a platonic friendship.

"You know, I'm so glad I never got involved with you," Ryan says to Crystal after he shares details of his hot but unfulfilling date with another woman. "I just would have ended up being some woman you had to get up out of bed and leave at 3 o'clock in the morning."

Crystal tells a male friend of his frank conversations with she's-just-my-pal Ryan, "The great thing is, I don't have to lie because I'm not always thinking about how get her into bed. I can just be myself."

After disappointments with other romances over years, Crystal and Ryan begin to wonder if they might be right for each other.

"I love that you get a little crinkle above your nose when you're looking at me like I'm nuts," Crystal tells Ryan in a climactic scene that captures some of her humorous quirks. "I love that you are the last person I want to talk to before I go to sleep at night and it's not because I'm lonely... I came here tonight because when you realize you want to spend the rest of your life with somebody, you want the rest of your life to start as soon as possible."

The dialog resonates because it expresses painful emotions bottled up inside audiences from their own real-life experiences. Ryan: "The first date back is always the toughest, Harry." Crystal: "Men and women can't be friends because the sex part always gets in the way." Ryan (sobbing about her ex-boyfriend): "All this time, I've been saying that he didn't want to get married. But, the truth is, he didn't want to marry me." Crystal: "If you're so over Joe, why aren't you seeing anyone?"

Those inspired lines came from Nora Ephron, who received the film's only Oscar nomination—for best original screenplay—and actors are credited with adding a few ad libs. The movie mostly takes place in New York City, the vastness of which provides an impersonal backdrop and enhances the soundtrack of big-city romantic tunes in a simple jazzy tone. A particularly daring touch that appears at various transitional points in the film are several brief interviews of elderly couples married for decades, recounting how their romances started.

1989
When Harry Met Sally...

Directed by ROB REINER

Starring: BILLY CRYSTAL (Harry Burns) MEG RYAN (Sally Albright)
CARRIE FISHER / BRUNO KIRBY

Music by MARC SHAIMAN

THE BOW-AND-ARROW OF CUPID COULDN'T HAVE TAKEN AIM AT A MORE UNLIKELY PAIRING: THE FUSSY, SLIGHTLY NEUROTIC BUT ADORABLE MEG RYAN AND THE WISE-CRACKING, SLIGHTLY CRUDE BUT PERCEPTIVE BILLY CRYSTAL.

«- Harry Burns (Billy Crystal):

I love that you get cold when it's 71 degrees out.
I love that it takes you an hour and a half to order a sandwich.
I love that you get a little crinkle above your nose when you're looking at me like I'm nuts.
I love that after I spend the day with you, I can still smell your

1. It wasn't exactly love-at-first-sight when Meg Ryan took a long-distance car ride with the boorish Billy Crystal when they were both in college, but their paths cross again years later and a strong, but platonic, friendship forms.

2. Meg Ryan delivers one of cinema's most hilarious scenes when out loud in a crowded restaurant she pretends to experience sexual pleasure to prove to an uncomfortable Billy Crystal that men don't know when women are just faking.

Crystal got top billing in the 1989 Columbia Pictures release that was produced by stylish indie filmmaker Castle Rock Entertainment. But the movie propelled Ryan, whose performance was mostly understated but with a few exuberant scenes, to a decade-long reign as Hollywood's top female star and "America's sweetheart" because she seemed like the-girl-next-door.

Though an instant hit, the film was unheralded with little pre-release buzz and its title was not settled even as late as principal photography. Among numerous other titles under consideration were "Harry, This Is Sally" and "How They Met."

Despite its sweetness, "When Harry Met Sally..." received a restrictive R rating for a few fleeting crude words describing sex and its famous fake orgasm scene. In that sequence, Crystal scoffs at Ryan's contention that women often pretend to have achieved sexual fulfillment in bed. To prove her point, Ryan begins writhing in a crowded restaurant, loudly moaning "oohs" and "oh yeah, right there."

Not surprisingly, Ryan's contrived over-the-top display of ecstasy shocks other patrons, leaving Crystal and cinema audiences to squirm with a combination of embarrassment and amusement. In the comedic capper to this memorable scene, an elderly woman—who is actually director Rob Reiner's real-life mother—tells a waitress as she nods toward Ryan, "I'll have what she's having."

He is a macho, young Wall Street banker who can't bring himself to ever say "I love you" even though he and his love know exactly how he feels.

When Patrick Swayze's character dies unexpectedly, "Ghost" tells the supernatural romantic tale of how his spirit lingers because that love is so strong. Swayze transforms into a friendly ghost protecting the love of his life, Demi Moore, who mourns his loss.

"I picked up your shirts today," Moore says talking out loud to herself just after Swayze's passing. "I don't know why...It's like I think about you every minute. It's like I can still feel you." Swayze's frustrated spirit is standing with her but she can't see or hear him (though the audience can).

While Swayze is a friendly ghost to Moore, he is a restless spirit because the circumstances surrounding his death trap him between the real world and heaven. Invisible to most characters in the movie, Swayze eventually masters the ability to move objects, which he uses to exact revenge. As one of his earthly tormenters realizes that Swayze's spirit is creating physical havoc, the unseen Swayze shouts with satisfaction, "Now do you believe in ghosts?"

The 1990 movie is generally considered a supernatural romance, but its range is really much broader. It touches on genres of genres are mystery, drama, chase, comedy, crime, thriller, and action adventure, and explores feelings of betrayal, passion, personal loss, exuberance, revenge, sentimentality, regret and deceit.

Of all these, humor is most pronounced, which is no surprise because "Ghost's" director is Jerry Zucker, who before this film was most associated with the wild physical comedy "Airplane!"

Most of the "Ghost's" humor is supplied by comedienne Whoopi Goldberg, who portrays a charlatan of a psychic who is shocked—and doesn't know how to react—when she actually does connect with someone from the spirit world. The flamboyant and street-wise Goldberg is perfectly cast as operator of a shady store front business with a sign saying, "Contact the dearly departed-$20."

The sassy and brassy shady lady eventually does the right thing even as Swayze's ghost turns her life upside down. "You are already dead," Goldberg shouts at Swayze as she tries to rid herself of the spirit that only she hears. "Why don't you just find a house to haunt, you know? Get some chains to rattle or something."

1990
Ghost

Directed by JERRY ZUCKER

Starring: PATRICK SWAYZE (Sam Wheat) DEMI MOORE (Molly Jensen)
WHOOPI GOLDBERG / TONY GOLDWYN

Music by MAURICE JARRE

PATRICK SWAYZE WRAPS HIS ARMS AROUND THE BACK OF DEMI MOORE AS SHE WORKS A POTTERY WHEEL, RESULTING IN BOTH THEIR FINGERS WORKING THE SQUISHY CLAY AS ONE. IT'S ONE OF CINEMA'S MOST SENSUAL SCENES, THANKS TO THE LATHERED UP CLAY.

▲ 1

Another particularly memorable scene shows a shirtless Swayze when still alive, wrapping himself around Moore's back as she works a pottery wheel. Together, they get their fingers lathered up in pottery clay in a coupling that is about as erotic as possible with two mostly-clothed people. Moore, who plays a sexy tomboy, then reverses by wrapping her legs around Swayze, putting them face-to-face for a passionate scene that helps earn "Ghost" its somewhat restrictive PG-13 audience classification. The 2 hour, 8 minute movie proved to be a box office sensation and received critical acclaim. "Ghost" received five Oscar nominations, including Best Picture, and won in two categories—Best Supporting Actress for Goldberg and Best Original Screenplay.

The supernatural scenes required extensive special effects, which are mostly good. Some critics knocked some of this screen magic being as uneven—particularly when some not-too-believable hooded demons collect the spirits of bad people moments after they die.

"Ghost" is famous in the movie business as a blockbuster built on gradual word-of-mouth buzz from audiences that convinced friends to see it. In its premiere weekend, "Ghost" opened inauspiciously at #2 but steadily grew box office clout in later weeks for an unusually long run in theaters, instead of a huge debut and a fast decline like most other blockbusters.

The Paramount Pictures-release finished the year as the #2 overall film while the movie that beat "Ghost" in its opening weekend—"Die Hard 2: Die Harder"—ended 1990 down at #8.

2

«-Sam Wheat:
People say "I love you" all the time,
and it doesn't mean anything.-»

1. Patrick Swayze can't believe his out-of-body experience as watches himself die on a city street after what seems to be a street robbery gone tragically wrong.

2. Demi Moore had sensed the presence of her dead love and for a moment Patrick Swayze becomes visible from the edge of the luminous spirit world for one last kiss goodbye. Swayze is restless ghost who is Moore's invisible protector when she's in jeopardy.

It may seem odd that this sweet fable of a love story in the mold of Cinderella received a restrictive R rating, but there's good reason with "Pretty Woman."

In the contemporary romantic comedy, Julia Roberts portrays a street prostitute who, by chance and with nothing to do with sex (at first anyway), ends up in the company of hard-driving businessman Richard Gere. Naturally, Gere softens like a ball of dough as he falls in love with her.

"I want more...I want the fairy tale," Roberts says softly to Gere as their love blossoms. When he later asks what happens when a knight in shining armor rescues a princess, Roberts says, "She rescues him right back." This moves Gere because he has struggled in his prior romantic relationships.

Taken at face value, "Pretty Woman" isn't believable because street-walker Roberts is portrayed as a happy, beautiful hooker who is emotionally better adjusted than most of the wealthy and privileged people around her. When two snooty wealthy women condescendingly suggest to Roberts that she is a gold-digger with her sights set on super-wealthy bachelor Gere, Roberts shoots back with a sassy, "Well, I'm not trying to land him. I'm just using him for sex."

Audiences look past the implausibility of it all because of such funny scenes and great screen chemistry between Gere and Roberts. Roberts received an Oscar nomination as best leading actress for the film's only Academy Award honor. Audiences are also captivated by erotic scenes of them in a bubble bath (which are highlighted in the film's promotion), their moments of passion and the visually-arresting transformation when Roberts replaces her trashy hooker clothes with elegant couture.

1990
Pretty Woman

Directed by GARRY MARSHALL

Starring: JULIA ROBERTS (Vivian Ward) RICHARD GERE (Edward Lewis)
RALPH BELLAMY / HECTOR ELIZONDO / JASON ALEXANDER / LAURA SAN GIACOMO

HIGH-POWERED BUSINESSMAN RICHARD GERE INITIALLY VIEWS CALL-GIRL JULIA ROBERTS AS JUST A PAID COMPANION, BUT SHE IS SEXY AND FUN TO BE AROUND, WHICH HAS GERE RETHINKING THE RELATIONSHIP. GERE IS AMAZED AT HOW JULIA ROBERTS LOOKS THE PART OF THE SOPHISTICATE WHEN SHE ACCOMPANIES HIM TO A POLO MATCH ATTENDED BY HIGH SOCIETY. SHE WORE TRASHY CLOTHING WHEN HE FIRST PICKED HER UP IN THE ROUGH PART OF TOWN.

«- Edward Lewis AMD Vivian Ward:
The question is how much more?
Vivian: I want the fairy tale.-»

1

2 ▲

1. Where Julia Roberts' character comes from, everyone uses plastic forks, so to prepare her for a fancy dinner, she needs instruction on the finer points of dining etiquette, which Hector Elizondo (standing) provides.

2. Wealthy businessman Gere presents a dolled-up Julia Roberts with a pricey necklace in this scene famous for him playfully snapping down the box lid as Roberts reaches for the jewelry.

The noteworthy supporting cast includes Jason Alexander—who at that time was starting to gain fame as a regular in the hit "Seinfeld" TV comedy and who portrays Gere's weasel of a corporate lawyer harassing Roberts. Hollywood golden era star Ralph Bellamy—then a recipient of a career achievement Oscar—plays an elderly businessman battling Gere.

Comedy director Garry Marshall—whose career is long on TV credits and a few noteworthy films—milks the premise for laughs. When Gere ushers her into an elevator at his swank hotel, Roberts—dressed in tight, short hot-pants and high sexy boots—scandalizes bystanders saying loudly, "Oh honey, you know what's happened? I got a 'runner' in my pantyhose. Oh, I'm not wearing pantyhose!"

The 1990 R-rated film with racy content came out at a pivotal historical turning point for its maker Walt Disney Studios, which only a few years earlier began diversifying from total reliance on wholesome family films. That diversification worked, because the film ranked a lofty fourth for the year at the box office.

"Beauty and the Beast" is the first animated film ever to be nominated for Best Picture Oscar, and the 1991 movie is one of only two works of animation to hold that distinction. That's because in 2001 the Academy of Motion Picture Arts & Sciences created a special category for Best Animated Feature, so it's unlikely Oscar voters will again choose an animated film to compete with live-action films in the overall best movie race.

In "Beauty and the Beast," pity poor Belle, who is a peasant girl in a French village circa 1700. Belle possesses a down-to-earth beauty with brown hair, brown eyes and a slim girlish figure, and she sings of wanting to escape village life in search of romance.

But her only prospects are the village's beefy, arrogant strongman Gaston, who wants to marry her, but is not very smart, and the Beast, who makes her a prisoner confined to his castle in exchange for freeing her father from his dungeon.

"Ohhh, isn't this amazing," sings Belle, referring to a novel she is reading before she becomes captive to the Beast. "It's my favorite part because, you'll see. Here's where she meets Prince Charming. But she won't discover that it's him. Till chapter three."

The Beast is a fearsome sight to behold. He is a hairy human-and-wolf-like creature with large ferocious teeth, small horns on his head and striking blue eyes. Often growling, he is prone to volcanic temper tantrums. While the Beast is physically intimidating, he mostly keeps his claw hands off those around him, and eventually, Belle coaxes some warmth from him.

Unknown to Belle, the Beast was once a handsome prince, who was put under a spell along with the people in his castle, who were transformed into animated household items. Those humans were turned into walking, talking "enchanted objects" such as a candelabra, feather duster, teapot, teacups and clock, but with human-like characteristics.

Daffy and chaotic, the enchanted objects advise the Beast on how to romance Belle, which will break the curse and turn them all back to normal humans. "And above all," two enchanted objects tell the Beast, "you must control your temper!" The audience can see by the look on his face that this befuddles the Beast.

1991
Beauty and the Beast

Directed by GARY TROUSDALE / KIRK WISE

Starring: PAIGE O'HARA (Belle) ROBBY BENSON (Beast)
RICHARD WHITE / ANGELA LANSBURY / JERRY ORBACH

Music by ALAN MENKEN / HOWARD ASHMAN

THE BEAUTIFUL BELLE, AND THE BEAST DANCE ALONE IN GRAND STYLE IN THE LARGE AND OPULENT BALLROOM OF HIS LONELY CASTLE. THE BEAST TRIES HIS BEST TO BE A COURTEOUS HOST AND MAKE BELLE COMFORTABLE. HE OFTEN ERUPTS INTO TIRADES AND IS ALWAYS IMPATIENT, BUT HAVING SWEET BELLE LIVE AT HIS LONELY CASTLE SEEMS TO BRING WARMTH TO HIS HEART.

▲ 1

The Beast gets off to an unpromising start in pursuit of Belle's heart. "You will join me for dinner," he says trying to be courtly, as one of the enchanted objects whispers encouragement in his ear. But then his temper gets the best of him when he shouts at Belle, "That's not a request!"

Over time, the Beast is warmed by Belle's friendliness and innocence, which diminish his outbursts of rage. Belle notices a change in the Beast as well. "But he's now different, Papa," she tells her amazed father. "He's changed somehow."

As part of the transformation, the Beast and Belle embrace for a waltz-like dance with sweeping elegance and an unexpected energy. In this magical scene, they turn and turn, dancing alone in a grand castle ballroom.

In the climatic ending of the film, love conquers all in breaking the curse on the Beast and the enchanted objects. Also, rough justice is dealt to the conniving suitor Gaston, who had whipped villagers into a frenzy to attack the Beast.

"Beauty and the Beast" was nominated for six Oscars for 1991, mostly in musical categories, winning for Original Score and Original Song. Its consideration for Best Picture was groundbreaking, though it did not win.

The well-known actors voicing roles in "Beauty and the Beast" are Robby Benson (voice of the Beast), Jerry Orbach, David Ogden Stiers and Angela Lansbury. But the 1 hour, 24 minute long G-rated (for General/all audience ages) Disney film does not have any Hollywood superstars that would pop up in popular animated films of later years.

"Beauty and the Beast" accelerated a trend of Disney creating substantial spinoffs to its newest full-length animated features. In this case, the movie spawned a popular Broadway stage play, two big-budget made-for-DVDs and a TV series.

«-The Beast and the prince:
You weren't made to be a servant. Even the floor longs
to be your mirror.-»

1. To free her father from the Beast's dungeon, Belle makes a deal promising to be the Beast's prisoner as the castle's "enchanted objects"—household items that can walk and talk—watch in the background.

2. The Beast lives in a castle without any humans in residence, but there is an odd assortment of "enchanted" objects such as candelabra and teapot that talk, and each have distinct personalities. The Beast looks scary and has a short temper, but underneath there seems to be a hidden soft side. Is there a human part of the Beast that is not visible?

Walt Disney Studios experienced a golden age of animation in the 1990s, with its 1992 musical romance "Aladdin" among its triumphs.

The adaptation of an Arabian folk tale has all the hallmarks of a full-length animated Disney film—great music, colorful visuals, a "princess" heroine, lively non-human characters and a diabolical villain, plus one other element that dazzles audiences.

Comedian and actor Robin Williams' frenetic voicing of the magic Genie character (who pops out of an oil lamp) elevates the movie further. His visual form transforms into a succession of characters, each with a distinctly different voice and presence. Many of Williams' voice imitations of celebrities are recognized only by adults who "get" the joke, but the rapid-fire speed and energy also enchants children who don't know the famous person.

"Once he's (Williams) out of that lamp, there's no stopping him," admired a "Washington Post" movie review. "You never know what's going to come out next."

While Williams as the Genie soars in "Aladdin," the basic story is driven by the plight of Princess Jasmine, who faces a deadline to find a husband within days or else have one selected by her father, the Sultan. "Father, I hate being forced into this," says Jasmine, providing a dose of modern feminism into a medieval tale by rejecting an arranged marriage. "If I do marry, I want it to be for love."

The Sultan's chief advisor, Jafar, provides the villainy as he plots to marry Jasmine so he can become Sultan. His chief henchman is a talking, human-like parrot Iago who enjoys plotting, which prompts this compliment from Jafar, "I love the way your foul little mind works." Many of Jafar's evil directives are delivered with a belly laugh of satisfaction.

Jasmine meets Aladdin, who is just poor street dweller, while she's on a brief and unauthorized excursion outside the palace walls. Though each makes a romantic impression on the other, they are soon pulled apart by outside forces. Then, Aladdin goes on a wild ride when he gains possession of the magic lamp whose Genie, portrayed by Williams, promises to fulfill three wishes.

"Well, there's this girl," Aladdin says slowly because he's obviously shy. "She's smart and fun and beautiful. She's got these eyes...and her smile, ahhh. But she's the princess. To even have a chance I'd have to be...hey, can you make me into a prince?"

PRINCESS JASMINE AND THE STREET-WISE WAIF ALADDIN TAKE A MAGIC CARPET RIDE WITH ALADDIN'S PET MONKEY ABU BARELY ABLE TO HANG ON TO THE BACK OF CARPET. WATCHING OVER THEM IS THE GENIE WHO SPRINKLES MAGIC IN THIS OLD ARABIAN FOLK TALE.

1992
Aladdin

Directed by RON CLEMENTS / JOHN MUSKER

Starring: SCOTT WEINGER (Aladdin) LINDA LARKIN (Jasmine) ROBIN WILLIAMS (Genie)
JONATHAN FREEMAN / FRANK WELKER

Music by ALAN MENKEN / HOWARD ASHMAN / TIM RICE

With magic from the Genie, Aladdin is transformed, and he presents himself to Jasmine as a real prince. One of Aladdin's struggles in the 1 hour, 30 minute movie is indecision on whether to keep up to pretense or reveal himself to Jasmine as the lowly street urchin she had met earlier.

When the Genie advises, "be yourself," Aladdin says dejectedly, "That's the last thing that I want to be." But battling the evil Jafar makes Aladdin more comfortable with himself and, anyway, Jasmine isn't so naïve not to notice.

"Aladdin" received five Oscar nominations, winning in two music categories. That's quite an achievement for a G-rated movie that was made to be suitable for audiences of all ages, since Academy Award voters generally gravitate to adult-oriented movies.

Some critics fault the romance between Aladdin and Jasmine as lackluster, in part since they share little screen time. There were also complaints that "Aladdin" contains stereotype characters, such as the Aladdin being a thief at the start of the film, and exaggerated facial features on other characters such as hooked noses that are unflattering. (It can be argued extreme characters are typical for all animation films).

Disney animators made Aladdin and Jasmine's facial features more European than most of the characters that surround them, which irks some film critics and audiences.

But overall, audiences didn't seem too bothered. "Aladdin" was the top grossing film of 1992, collecting a Sultan's treasure of $217 million from cinema tickets in North America and $504 million on a worldwide basis.

Really just a commoner, Aladdin gets transformed into a prince through a magical spell so he can woo Princess Jasmine. Will she notice he's the same lad dressed in tattered clothes with whom she once shared a chance meeting outside the palace?

Is it pre-ordained that two people are always meant for each other and fate will unite them? Meg Ryan's character in "Sleeping in Seattle" thinks so. But as she follows her heart in pursuit of a lonely widower, played by Tom Hanks, she becomes less sure.

In the romantic comedy, Ryan—dubbed "America's sweetheart" by film critics for her natural-looking beauty—gets hung up on destiny after her mother recalls the first time she met her husband, which came completely by accident. "Then he held my hand...and I knew," mother tells her daughter. Ryan, who is hanging on every word, asks Mom, "Knew what?"

"You know...magic," replies her mother. "It was magic... I knew we'd be together forever and everything would be wonderful."

Ryan is engaged to be married to Bill Pullman, but wonders why she hasn't come under the spell of that magic. She becomes even more conflicted when she feels inexplicably drawn to Hanks after hearing him speak emotionally on a national radio talk show about his emptiness after his wife died young.

To keep his privacy, the radio talk show hostess identifies Hanks simply as Sleepless in Seattle. His poignant words creates a sensation with the public and the radio station forwards to Hanks hundreds of letters from women listeners, including one from Ryan, though his identity turns out to be a not-so-well-kept secret.

Ryan—who is on the other side of the continent in Baltimore—and her co-workers discuss Hanks' comments the next day. "This kid calls up and says 'my dad needs a wife,'" Ryan says. After Hanks' son coaxes him to the phone, Ryan adds, "I was listening him to talk about how much he loved his wife and suddenly I was crying."

Weeping is fixture of the film, though in a comedic vein. Ryan and a friend sob watching 1957 the Cary Grant tear-jerker, "An Affair to Remember" on TV. With its intentionally over-done moments of manufactured romantic tragedy, "Sleepless in Seattle" is a women's film, but it's a chick flick guys can like because much of its comedy plays to both genders.

1993
Sleepless in Seattle

Directed by NORA EPHRON

Starring: TOM HANKS (Sam Baldwin) MEG RYAN (Annie Reed)
BILL PULLMAN / ROSS MALINGER / ROSIE O'DONNELL

Music by MARC SHAIMAN

«-Annie Reed:
Destiny is something we've invented
because we can't stand the fact that
everything that happens is accidental.-»

Hanks teases another female character about her hanky-dabbing reaction to "An Affair to Remember" with pretend sobbing, while saying, "I cried (too) at the end of the 'Dirty Dozen'...Trini Lopez busted his neck while they were parachuting down
behind the Nazi lines." But for most of the film, Hanks is a noble though wounded single parent.

As "Sleepless in Seattle" reaches its finale on the observation deck of the Empire State Building in New York—which par-
allels "An Affair to Remember"—Ryan suddenly finds courage to break off her engagement to Pullman and then immediately
sees a sign she follows to Hanks. The audience knows exactly where the plot is heading and this PG-13 film gets there quickly
with its brisk 1 hour, 45 minute running time.

The 1993 Sony Pictures release received two Oscar nominations including best original screenplay. The supporting cast
delivered memorable performances including Pullman, comedienne Rosie O'Donnell, Rob Reiner (he also directed the romantic comedy hit "When Harry Met Sally..." starring Ryan), Hanks' wife Rita Wilson and impish straight-man David Hyde Pierce.

Hanks and Ryan were already Hollywood stars when "Sleepless in Seattle" became 1993's most popular romantic comedy, which was much improved from their previous pairing three years earlier in "Joe Versus the Volcano." The duo would hit
box office jackpot again in 1998 with "You've Got Mail." Though neither Hanks nor Ryan received Oscar attention for "Sleepless
in Seattle," Hanks would win his first Academy Award for his lead drama role in "Philadelphia" released the same year.

The movie is a slice of life from the early 1990s. Call-in talk radio is all the rage, Ryan's character searches for Hanks on
a pre-Internet office computer, and Celine Dion, Carly Simon and Joe Cocker songs are on the movie's soundtrack. The eclec-
tic movie music album—which also includes old love song standards, soft jazz and cool piano—was a big hit along with the film.

1. After Tom Hank's wife dies, he plays a doting, but heartbroken single dad to his son, portrayed by Ross Malinger. His son schemes to find him another love after realizing there's emptiness in his father's life.

2. Meg Ryan, who reigned as America's Sweetheart in Hollywood movies during the 1990s, portrays a character who obsesses about romantic relationships and marriage when talking with a gal pal on the phone.

Love, betrayal, brotherhood, suspense, bloody gore and Hollywood stars fill the screen in "Legends of the Fall." Anthony Hopkins and Brad Pitt carry this period epic, that is a generational drama and romance set in Montana over the decades starting in 1913.

While Hopkins and Pitt—whose characters are father and son—are top billed, the story really revolves around Julia Ormond, who becomes romantically connected to all three of Hopkins' sons at the isolated ranch. A sense of tragedy weighs on Ormond as she writes a letter to one brother for whom she longs, but who left her at the Montana ranch to travel the world searching for adventure.

"I have nowhere to send this letter," Ormond's voiceover says, "and no reason to believe that you wish to receive it. I wrote it only for myself. And so I will hide it away along with all the things left unsaid and undone between us."

The big sky scenery, sweeping symphonic music and reliance on horses for travel convey the feel of old-fashioned Westerns from the 1940s and 1950s. Plus, there's a narration sprinkled with naturalistic and mystical allegories provided by native-American actor Gordon Tootoosis, who also is seen in the movie.

But any similarities with old-fashioned Hollywood Westerns are just on the surface because "Legends of the Fall" is more complex, coarser, and the romantic intrigue is painfully deep. For example, a crude word for sex helps garner a restrictive R-rating for the 1994 release by Sony Pictures' TriStar banner. Also, a few brief scenes of passion, although not excessively revealing, show characters undressed.

Pitt is the wild and irresponsible son, yet he's the most sympathetic male character. Family patriarch Hopkins is noble, but he's disgusted with the world and brooding—mainly from regrets of having fought native Indians years earlier while a colonel in the U.S. Army. His other two sons have flaws: the eldest, who is portrayed by Aidan Quinn, is a conniver, and youngest, played by Henry Thomas, is naïve and bookish.

1994
Legends of the Fall

Directed by EDWARD ZWICK

Starring: BRAD PITT (Tristan Ludlow) JULIA ORMOND (Susannah Fincannon Ludlow)
ANTHONY HOPKINS / AIDAN QUINN / HENRY THOMAS

Music by JAMES HORNER

BRAD PITT IS THE WILD CHILD OF HIS FAMILY AT THEIR RANCH IN MONTANA IN THE EARLY 1900S. WOMEN FIND HIM ATTRACTIVE BUT THEY KNOW HE'S NOT THE DEPENDABLE TYPE WHO WILL LIVE A SETTLED-DOWN LIFE.

"Tristan (Pitt), you know you can't make her happy," a resigned Quinn says to Pitt about Ormond. Pitt responds, "Gotta try." Quinn then says slowly to convey a certainty, "You will fail."

Quinn himself is a spurned suitor pursuing Ormond, who is a beauty with square features and bushy, flowing brown hair. "I think you know that I'm in love with you," Quinn says awkwardly while standing alone with Ormond at his family's cemetery. "From the first moment I saw you, like in a novel."

Ormond smiles nervously and looks uncomfortable, like she wants to be somewhere else as Quinn continues. "Is there any hope that you could learn to love me? Enough to," he says as his voice trails off. "Susannah (Ormond), we could make a life together. A happy life." Orman answers softly "I don't think so, Alfred (Quinn)."

1. Three brothers grow up in a tightly-knit family on a remote Montana ranch in the early 1900s (from left)—the pragmatic Aidan Quinn, the naively idealistic Henry Thomas, and the rough-and-ready Brad Pitt.

2. Anthony Hopkins is the patriarch of a family in the early 20th century American West, who wants isolation from mainstream society, after being disgusted by the government's cruel treatment of the Native American population. His three sons don't all share his values.

▼ 1

1

"Legends of the Fall" is based on a slim novella by Jim Harrison yet provides more than enough story to fill the sprawling 2 hour, 12 minute movie. As the film unfolds, the audience is left hanging as to how the Ormond love story will play out because there are so many unexpected twists and turns.

The open West (actually mostly Canadian landscape) contributed to the film's one Oscar win—in cinematography. "Legends of the Fall" was also nominated for two other Academy Awards in sound and art/set decoration.

Two talents behind the camera weren't nominated but have Oscar pedigrees. Director Edward Zwick would win an Oscar for his later work on "Shakespeare in Love." The creator of the original music in "Legends of the Fall," James Horner, went on to win two Oscars for music in block-buster "Titanic."

Look closely at Thomas to see the actor who was the child star who memorably found the friendly alien 12 years earlier in "E.T. – The Ex-tra-Terrestrial."

1. Julia Ormond shares a tender kiss with strapping Brad Pitt in a secluded spot on the family's ranch. She's also romantically involved with his two brothers at various times.

2. Romantically involved with three brothers, Julia Ormond ends up marrying the least likely of the three—Aidan Quinn, who emerges as a wealthy businessman and powerful government official, though at the cost of his integrity.

IT WAS THOSE WHO LOVED HIM MOST WHO DIED YOUNG. HE WAS A ROCK THEY BROKE THEMSELVES AGAINST HOWEVER MUCH HE TRIED TO PROTECT THEM.

Walt Disney's 33rd full-length animated film that was released in 1995, "Pocahontas" has a central princess character like many other Disney cartoons, although this story differs in that she has two love interests.

The 1995 movie tells of a love story between a Native American woman and John Smith, an English settler who helped found Jamestown, Virginia. Pocahontas is set for a marriage arranged by her father to a warrior from her tribe when the British show up unexpectedly in 1607.

"Why do all my dreams extend," the Pocahontas character sings. "Just around the river bend; For a handsome sturdy husband; Never dreams that something might be coming." That signature music is sung by noted Broadway stage singer Judy Kuhn.

John Smith's character is voiced by Oscar-winner Mel Gibson. "Pocahontas, look at me," Gibson tells her in a private moment, while imprisoned by her tribe and facing execution. "I'd rather die tomorrow than live a hundred years without knowing you... No matter what happens to me, I'll always be with you, forever."

The movie is unusual for a Disney animated film because it is loosely based on real history—a celebrated romance involving the Indian princess and an early settler. Not an easy-to-tell fairy tale like other Disney animated movies, "Pocahontas" was still a hit at the box office, despite a core story lacking an unambiguously evil villain. However, the thick-headed and gold-crazed British colonists provide some wickedness for the film.

"Remember what awaits us there," the leader of the settlers, voiced by David Ogden Stiers tells the crew when sailing to the New World. "Freedom, prosperity, the adventure of our lives...nothing, not wind nor rain or nor 1,000 blood thirsty savages shall stand in our way!"

The absence of intense evil helped the 1 hour, 21 minute film secure a G audience classification as suitable for all ages.

1995
Pocahontas

Directed by MIKE GABRIEL / ERIC GOLDBERG

Starring: IRENE BEDARD and JUDY KUHN (Pocahontas) MEL GIBSON (John Smith)
DAVID OGDEN STIERS / RUSSELL MEANS / LINDA HUNT

Music by ALAN MENKEN

A ENGLISH SETTLER, VOICED BY MEL GIBSON, IS CAPTIVATED BY NATIVE AMERICAN POCAHONTAS, WHO HAS SOME ENCHANTING FRIENDS—GRANDMOTHER ▲
WILLOW (A TALKING TREE), A PLAYFUL RACCOON NAMED MEEKO AND A HUMMINGBIRD FLIT. THE PUG DOG PERCY CAME WITH THE BRITISH.

Being a Disney production, the story is idealistic and there are plenty of elements of fantasy. A raccoon and humming bird accompany Pocahontas everywhere like house pets. Providing some critter humor, the raccoon, Meeko, amusingly gets stuck at the opposite end of the same log as pug-breed dog named Percy who arrives with the British. In another touch of Disney story magic, any language barrier between Indians and the English quickly disappears when everyone conveniently speaks in English. And a wise old tree named Grandmother Willow is human-like and talks, dispensing sage advice. "Listen," the tree, voiced by Oscar-winner Linda Hunt tells Pocahontas. "All around you are spirits, child.

Pocahontas needs all the advice she can get, because her tribe and the British settlers are itching for a fight over control of the land. The newcomers are technologically more advanced, but imperious and dismissive of the Indians, who are portrayed as noble and wise because they are in touch with and have respect for nature.

So a backdrop behind the love story is a clash of cultures. "You think I'm an ignorant savage," Pocahontas sings. "How can there be so much that you don't know?"

Of course, the Indians aren't completely perfect because they have one flaw in common with the English—suspicion of strangers. "They're different than us, which means they can't be trusted," an Indian proclaims in song as he prepares for war with the British.

"Pocahontas" won two Oscars for its music, and the theatrical film spawned a successful 1998 direct-to-DVD spinoff "Pocahontas II: Journey to a New World" in which the title character goes to London. That story is loosely based on true events, because the real Pocahontas went to England. But unlike in Disney's version, she died as a young adult of unknown causes.

▲ 1

I'd rather die tomorrow than live a hundred years without knowing you.

1. When English settlers arrive in the New World in 1607 on big sailing ships, Native American princess Pocahontas faces the tough choice of whether to follow the advice of her Indian tribe and avoid the newcomers or to listen to her heart when she strikes up a romance with a settler.

2. Pocahontas continues a long line of "princess" characters that are central to many of Walt Disney's full-length animated theatrical films; they are admirable and true-hearted, which is fortunate because events always test them and they must look within themselves for the courage they didn't know was there.

A professional photographer lost while on assignment to shoot historic covered bridges in rural Iowa in the 1960s asks directions from a middle-aged housewife alone on an isolated farm.

"The Bridges of Madison County" starts with a lot of small talk, but audiences know where this meandering 2 hour, 15 minute-long romantic drama is headed. Clint Eastwood portrays a divorced loner who travels the world as a photographer and meets Streep, who lives an anchored life with her husband and two children, all of whom are out of town for a few days.

When Eastwood asks about life in Iowa, Streep fidgets and answers, "Oh, it's just fine. It's quiet and the people are real nice. And all that's true, mostly. It is quiet." Streep, who character was born in Italy and married a U.S. soldier who brought her to the farm, then adds matter-of-factly while looking away, "It's not what I dreamed of as a girl."

Streep assumes her role so convincingly as a still-pretty but fading war-bride housewife trapped in a bland existence, that audiences quickly forget they're watching Meryl Streep. When Eastwood unexpectedly shows up she's dowdy, but quickly changes her hairdo and clothes to achieve a subdued sexiness. Streep was nominated for an Oscar in the only Academy Award nod for this 1995 release from Warner Bros.

After small talk is replaced by passion, Eastwood probes where their relationship will go. Streep captures the essence of the practical woman with this controlled response: "To do what? Go off with someone who needs everyone but no one in particular. I mean, what would be the point" as Streep flashes a momentary smile to herself. She then continues, "Would you pass the butter please?"

Streep's marital status makes the PG 13-rated "Bridges of Madison County" what Hollywood calls a "weeper" because it's a sad melodrama that drives audiences to tears. Streep may be unhappy in her marriage, but she remains loyal to her family, so there will be no happily-ever-after with Eastwood.

1995

The Bridges of Madison County

Directed by CLINT EASTWOOD

Starring: CLINT EASTWOOD (Robert Kincaid)   MERYL STREEP (Francesca Johnson)

Music by LENNIE NIEHAUS

CLINT EASTWOOD IS A PROFESSIONAL PHOTOGRAPHER WITH CAMERA BAG SLUNG OVER HIS SHOULDER WHO BY CHANCE MEETS MERYL STREEP—A FARMER'S WIFE IN RURAL IOWA—WHEN HE GETS LOST. STREEP PORTRAYS AN ITALIAN WOMAN WHO LIVES A QUIET LIFE AS HOUSEWIFE IN MIDDLE AMERICA, YEARS MARRYING AN AMERICAN SOLDIER.

The movie is told in flashback as Streep's adult children learn of her infidelity from a review of her personal effects after her death. Piling on the melodramatic sorrow, Streep's grown kids discuss with each other their own marital failures, after first being shocked by evidence of their mother's infidelity years earlier when they were children.

Two touches in "Bridges of Madison County" show the imprint of Eastwood, who was director as well as male lead. Romantic scenes are filmed in low light, conveying a dark feeling. Another atmospheric touch is a simple melancholy music track often just soft piano and simple jazz—which are Eastwood's favorites.

Critics praised the movie for providing more texture to the characters than the book on which it was based, which was knocked for its flat writing despite a fascinating plot. In the movie, Streep's character has a playful streak and the macho Eastwood shows some intriguing soft edges.

Some film critics compare this movie to "Lawrence of Arabia," but the only similarity is its sweeping cinematic shots of epic desert vistas.

"The English Patient" is really a mystery with two intertwined romantic dramas that moves slowly on a vast landscape of World War II-era North Africa and Italy. The movie has enigmatic characters with murky pasts, some of which unexpectedly converge as the film unfolds via numerous flashbacks.

"You're in love with him, aren't you?" Allied forces spy and spy catcher Willem Dafoe sneers at military hospital nurse Juliette Binoche, referring to badly-burned Ralph Fiennes. "Your poor patient. You think he's a saint because of the way he looks? I don't think he is."

In flashbacks, Fiennes is seen as a robust adventurer mapping North Africa, who has a torrid affair with married Kristin Scott Thomas, a lanky blonde siren, whether outfitted in desert fatigues or in a dress for a formal dinner in Cairo. Their steamy scenes of passion—some of them wordless—helped earn "The English Patient" a restrictive R audience classification.

Like the WWII backdrop, the cast is multinational: Fiennes, Naveen Andrews, Thomas and Thomas' screen husband Colin Firth are British; Binoche is French; and Dafoe is American (though Fiennes, Andrews, Binoche and Dafoe portray other nationalities in the film).

Besides intrigue, there is tragedy. A character in a love triangle, mortally injured when a lover takes revenge in the desert, writes these dying words that are found by the third, who comes to the rescue too late: "My darling. I'm waiting for you. The fire is gone now, and I'm horribly cold. We die (with)...fears we've hidden in—like this wretched cave." This poignant goodbye is cleverly revealed at the end of the film, long after the words were written.

1996
The English Patient

Directed by ANTHONY MINGHELLA

Starring: RALPH FIENNES (Count László Almásy)   KRISTIN SCOTT THOMAS (Katharine Clifton)
JULIETTE BINOCHE / WILLEM DAFOE / NAVEEN ANDREWS / COLIN FIRTH

Music by GABRIEL YARED

THE TRUE IDENTITY OF RALPH FIENNES'S CHARACTER SEEMS A BIT MURKY, BUT NOT SO FOR KRISTIN SCOTT THOMAS. SHE'S MARRIED TO AN ENGLISHMAN YET ATTRACTED TO FIENNES WHEN THEY MEET IN NORTH AFRICA AT THE OUTSET OF THE WORLD WAR II.

"The English Patient" won nine Academy Awards, including Best Picture for 1996, making it one of the honored films in Oscar history. Besides Best Picture, the film earned a Best Director award for Anthony Minghella and Best Supporting Actress for Binoche. "The English Patient" received a total of 12 Oscar nominations. The movie is based on the novel by Canadian writer Michael Ondaatje, who was born in Sri Lanka.

Though the film won all those Oscars, some fault "The English Patient" for structural deficiencies, in addition to its slow-to-unfold pace. Binoche's character is said to be good to the point of being saintly, and thus lacks nuances.

The Fiennes character is hard for audiences to make a personal connection with. He is seen either as a static burn patient confined to bed, or in flashbacks as a dour traveling companion who periodically erupts into strange rants. When Thomas breaks off their affair in one flashback scene, Fiennes calls after her with this bizarre farewell, "I just want you to know; I'm not missing you yet."

But the acting performances and visuals—the desert landscapes are beautiful in their desolation from the vantage of flying airplanes—are universally acclaimed as magnificent. The movie was filmed in Italy and Tunisia.

Ralph Fiennes writes in a North African desert with his party's camp in background. He's in the British zone in World War II, though his allegiances are not clear.

"The English Patient" cost somewhere between $27-31 million to film, which was a bargain given its period WWII setting that included some battle scenes, and its longish 2 hour 42 minute running length. At the time, the average production cost of a major studio movie stood at $40 million.

The movie started out at 20th Century Fox, which pulled out at the last minute reportedly because it preferred different actors in some roles and wanted to shave the production budget. Miramax Films—which an independent studio (though owned by Walt Disney Studios)—came to the rescue.

"The English Patient's" award glory added to Miramax's impressive Oscar pedigree, that includes "Shakespeare in Love," "Chicago" and "The Crying Game." There's also another Oscar connection with its producer Saul Zaentz, an American music impresario who produced other Best Picture Academy Award winners "One Flew Over the Cuckoo's Nest" and "Amadeus."

Kristin Scott Thomas is an English beauty who complicates her life with an extra martal affair when travelling with her husband in North Africa just as World War II is about to start.

When the Titanic catastrophically sank in 1912, the panic on the mammoth luxury ocean liner brought out the best and worst of those on board who were all desperate to survive. The 1997 movie named for the ship presents the catastrophe with historical accuracy through a fictional love affair between two passengers, portrayed by Leonardo DiCaprio and Kate Winslet.

Their rendezvous with history gives the romance in "Titanic" plenty of drama. When clinging to floating debris and each other in the frigid North Atlantic Ocean after their ship sinks, a shivering Winslet keeps her fire burning by vowing to DiCaprio, "I'll never let go, Jack. I promise."

The star-crossed lovers are among the admirable souls in the catastrophe. But Winslet's snobbish fiancée—portrayed by Billy Zane—is a villain who uses his wealth and deception to secure a seat on one of the few available lifeboats.

The youth audience—which is usually cool to historical dramas—was the first wave in the box office stampede, captivated by the screen romance between DiCaprio—then mostly known as a TV actor—and British actress Winslet—who portrayed an American. The romantic drama propelled both to instant international stardom.

"Titanic's" drama revolves around the Winslet character, who is pushed to marry for money but falls for the brash, working-class DiCaprio. The movie is framed in a flashback through Winslet's character, who as an old woman many years later opens up about this lost chapter of her life: "He saved me in every way that a person can be saved. I don't even have a picture of him," she says with a sorrow and slowness that comes with age. "He exists now only in my memory."

Upon its release, "Titanic" had the distinction of being both the most expensive film ever made (in absolute dollars) and the highest grossing film of all time. The romantic drama's signatures are its music, which is both haunting and soaring, and the famous scene of an exuberant DiCaprio standing on bow of the mighty ship shouting, "I am the king of the world. Wa-hoo!" He returns to that perch to stand together with Winslet.

1997
Titanic

Directed by JAMES CAMERON

Starring: KATE WINSLET (Rosalinda "Rose" DeWitt Bukater), LEONARDO DICAPRIO (Jack Dawson)

KATE WINSLET IS SURPRISED AND ENCHANTED WITH THE FASHION MAKEOVER OF LEONARDO DICAPRIO, WHEN HE BORROWS FORMAL CLOTHES FOR A POSH DINNER ABOARD THE TITANIC OCEAN LINER. THEY ARE SAILING TO AN UNCERTAIN DESTINY IN 1912."

«-Jack: Where to, Miss?
-Rose: To the stars.-»

2 ▲

Writer/director James Cameron didn't let the impressive special effects—some of which he helped invent specially for "Titanic"—eclipse the human story. The camera moves through elaborate period settings, giving the audience a feeling of you-are-there, and suspense builds even as audiences know that an iceberg and tragedy ultimately lurk around the corner.

The historical drama helped provide the gravitas to win the Oscar for Best Picture, which was among the film's 11 Academy Awards from a total of 14 nominations.

But "Titanic" has detractors who complain that at its core the film is an unremarkable melodrama. They say it is much too convenient that DiCaprio's working-class character ascends from steerage to first class to woo Winslet, and that she is merely a poor little rich girl. Further, critics knock the love story and villains as one-dimensional, but others say this simplicity is an attribute, given the large and busy historical backdrop of the film.

1. and 2. It's 1912 as young lovers Leonardo DiCaprio and Kate Winslet stand on a forward position of one of the wonders of the new Industrial Age—the majestic, huge and unsinkable Titanic ocean liner. It seems nothing could possibly go wrong for them on their voyage.

As the mighty Titanic quickly starts to sink, passengers including Leonardo DiCaprio and Kate Winslet are going to be tossed into the frigid North Atlantic Ocean with only debris to cling to.

The PG-13-rated movie experienced massive costs overruns from its orig-
nal $125 million production budget (optimistically too low) to an over-the-t
$235 million final filming cost—though this figure is not confirmed. With a th
atrical running time of 3 hours 14 minutes, it's twice as long as a normal film.

Months before the movie reached theaters, critics unleashed a barrage
bad press citing its bloated cost and using various maritime metaphors to pred
a box office disaster. Despite the bad buzz, audiences became curious as to wh
Hollywood's most expensive film looked like splashed on the silver screen. In t
end, filmmaker Cameron, Paramount Pictures (US/Canada distributor) and 20
Century Fox (international distributor that originated the film) got the last laug
"Titanic" grossed $1.8 billion worldwide at theaters, smashing all record
Cameron went on to achieve similar success with his big-budget "Avatar" in 200

«-Jack Dawson:
Promise me you'll survive. That you
won't give up, no matter what
happens, no matter how hopeless.
Promise me now, Rose, and never let
go of that promise.-»

For decades, the literary elite savored film versions of Shakespeare's weightier works, such as Hamlet, Macbeth, and King Lear. Then in 1998, along came the light-hearted "Shakespeare in Love," a movie that played to a much wider audience and that was showered with Oscars. Very little is known about The Great Bard as a real-life person, and the Universal/Miramax movie invents a romantic experience that might have shaped William Shakespeare's works when he was just an up-and-comer in Elizabethan England's hardscrabble stage world.

When the loan-shark moneyman behind a play asks who the young man is addressing everyone during a rehearsal, the producer answers in a dismissive tone, "Nobody...it's the author," referring to the playwright who now is considered the world's foremost literary figure.

At first, those rehearsals look unpromising for a comedy provisionally titled, "Romeo and Ethel the Pirate's Daughter." But because of an ill-fated off-stage romance, Joseph Fiennes—who portrays Shakespeare—completely revises the play to the uber-tragedy that the world today reveres as "Romeo and Juliet."

Seen as an intense young playwright struggling to carve out a place in the world, Fiennes battles writers block, poverty and harassment from a powerful nobleman who is his lover's other suitor. That love interest is played by Gwyneth Paltrow, who portrays a noble woman who becomes Fiennes' artistic muse and inspiration. Through quick cuts, the movie shows them reciting freshly-penned dialog while frolicking between the sheets.

Fair-maiden Paltrow shows a passion for genuine love in an era of arranged, loveless marriages, like the one she faces, and she also is enthralled by stage plays. "All the men at court are without poetry," laments Paltrow, who is like an imprisoned princess because theater is frowned upon as low-class in her Elizabethan circle of high society. "I will have poetry in my life. And adventure. And love, love above all. Love that overthrows life...come ruin or rapture."

1998
Shakespeare
in Love

IT'S SHOWTIME AT THE ROSE THEATRE IN LONDON IN THE 1593, WHERE GWYNETH PALTROW IS AN EMERGENCY REPLACEMENT CAST MEMBER. HERE SHE EMBRACES THE YOUNG PLAYWRIGHT AND ACTOR PORTRAYED BY JOSEPH FIENNES, WITH WHOM SHE SECRETLY PURSUES A ROMANCE. THE AUDIENCE IN THE BACKGROUND IS ENTHRALLED BY THE PLAY.

«-Viola:
I am afeared. Being in night,
all this is but a dream. -»

▲ 1

KR 12

Just as in "Romeo and Juliet," Fiennes secretly comes to her balcony when they are smitten. Like the famous play, theirs is a strong
love that the forces around them turn into a tragedy. The movie ends
with them unexpectedly performing "Romeo and Juliet" together on
stage and enthralling a standing-room-only audience. It turns out that
street-wise Queen Elizabeth—portrayed by Judi Dench—is in the audience and she provides this perceptive comment about how the intrigue
around her ends "as stories must when love's denied: with tears and a

1. Colin Firth portrays a conniving aristocrat who in court intrigue tries to impress Queen Elizabeth played by Judi Dench. His character intends to marry into much-needed money to fuel his ambitions.

2. Gwyneth Paltrow is an aristocrat who loves a commoner playwright. But, when pressed by her family, marries a nobleman from her own class, portrayed by Colin Firth.

«-Elizabeth I:
Playwrights teach us nothing about love.
They make it pretty; they make it comical;
or they make it lust. They cannot make it true.-»

He's probably the most disgusting leading man in the history of cinema: bad breath, grumpy, ugly and he scratches his butt in public.

But the 2001 full-length animated movie "Shrek" was a hit around the world and winner of the Oscar for Best Animated Feature Film, in what was the first year for that Oscar category. The romantic comedy was also nominated for Best Adapted Screenplay in competition with all films, not just animated movies.

"Shrek" takes place in a mythical medieval world with castles, men carrying swords and shields, strange creatures in the forest (like Shrek) and magic spells.

Princess Fiona, who is voiced by actress Cameron Diaz, is an indefatigable romantic when a knight wearing a helmet rescues her from a dragon's lair. "Sir Knight, this beeth our first meeting," the Princess says using a touch of archaic English language, "should it not be a wonderful, romantic moment? You should sweep me off my feet." The knight shrugs off this romantic opportunity and instead pulls her by the arm, saying "Jah, sorry lady. There's no time."

Though she doesn't know who's under the helmet (or perhaps more correctly what's under the helmet), the audience realizes that it the green-colored ogre Shrek, who is voiced by Mike Myers with a Scottish accent.

When Shrek finally removes the helmet, the Princess is taken aback. While the ogre is comfortable with his green skin, home in a grimy swamp and bad personal habits, he laments that others shun him and, even worse, sometimes attack him for no reason other than his looks.

"It's the world that seems to have a problem with me," complains Shrek, who is big and cloddish but resourceful and sensible, though that often gets lost by his impatience with those around him. "People take one look at me and go, 'Aaah, help, run! Big stupid ogre.' They judge me before they even know me."

After Shrek rescues the Princess, they go on a long journey to a castle where she is supposed to marry the ruler. But along the way, they develop feelings for each other and the Princess turns out to have a secret—she's not just a helpless damsel in distress. This secret means that she is more compatible with Shrek than he first realizes.

SOME MIGHT THINK TWO GREEN OGRES KISSING WOULD BE UGLY, BUT IT'S A BEAUTIFUL SIGHT FOR THE OPPRESSED RESIDENTS OF A MEDIEVAL KINGDOM WHERE SHREK AND FIONA'S UNLIKELY PAIRING CONTRIBUTES TO THE TOPPLING OF THEIR CRUEL RULER.

2001
Shrek

Directed by ANDREW ADAMSON / VICKY JENSON

Starring: MIKE MYERS (Shrek) / CAMERON DIAZ (Princess Fiona)
EDDIE MURPHY / JOHN LITHGOW / VINCENT CASSEL

Music by HARRY GREGSON-WILLIAMS / JOHN POWELL

Some critics say wisecracking comic Eddie Murphy outshines everyone as Shrek's sidekick. Murphy voices a talking donkey who carries on in rapid-fire modern urban language and—in what sets up numerous jokes—frequently goes into a panic. When a dragon turns out to be a female who takes a liking to Donkey (the character has no other name), he plays the cool modern dude telling her, "I'm kinda old fashioned. I don't want to rush into a... physical relationship... I'm not that emotionally ready for a... uh... commitment of this... uh... magnitude!"

That dialog makes fun of contemporary dating relationship jabber, which makes "Shrek" so delightful to sophisticated audiences. The 1 hour, 30 minute film is packed with wicked jokes that make adults laugh while kids probably don't understand the contemporary connections. But children still find enough slapstick, adventure, romance and visual excitement on the screen to be highly entertained.

"Shrek" carried a mildly restrictive PG rating for small bits of off-color humor. Critics praised its animation as top-rate, with creatures that seem lifelike with authentic eye movement, shadows, and realistic skin flexing with body action.

The movie blossomed into a long-running franchise that is a cornerstone of DreamWorks Animation SKG, which emerged as the only consistent rival to Walt Disney Animation Studios and its Pixar Animation Studios. "Shrek" inspired numerous media spinoffs including sequel movies, video games and Broadway-style stage shows.

2

« - Fiona:
You didn't slay the dragon?
 - Shrek:
It's on my to-do list. Now come on! -»

1. Princess Fiona (voiced by Cameron Diaz), Shrek (Mike Myers) and the talking Donkey (Eddie Murphy) journey to within sight of the castle where she is to marry the lord of the realm, although on their journey Fiona becomes attached to the homely but heroic ogre Shrek.

2. After a battle with marauders in the forest, Shrek is surprised to find an arrow sticking out of his buttocks. Princess Fiona proves resourceful in extracting this arrow from his butt and she was capable in the earlier fight, which foreshadows that she is no ordinary princess.

238-239 Princess Fiona and the ogre Shrek are quite an unlikely couple, secretly, she knows she is more like Shrek than he realizes.

Romantic comedy "My Big Fat Greek Wedding" is famous in Hollywood as a gigantic "sleeper hit" that was completely unheralded when it first landed in theaters and also the film's pedigree is famous.

For its opening weekend in April 2002, "My Big Fat Greek Wedding" ranked a lowly #20 among all films in theaters. But the light comedy about a cross-cultural romance that rocks an immigrant Greek family in Chicago resonated with audiences. Favorable reviews from film critics and word-of-mouth from audiences recommending the movie to their friends drew ever-larger crowds. At the end of the year, the low-budget, $5 million independent film finished a lofty fifth in box office—putting it in the company of studio blockbusters that cost tens of millions of dollars to make.

As for its pedigree, the romantic comedy was co-produced by Oscar-winning actor Tom Hanks and his wife Rita Wilson (though they do not appear on screen).

In "My Big Fat Greek Wedding," Nia Vardalos stars as a 30-something woman working in her family restaurant, where she is down-hearted because she unmarried. Her character—who sheds her frumpy demeanor after a cosmetic makeover—comes to life when she dates and then gets engaged to a nice local guy. But there's one big problem—he's an American without even a drop of Greek blood.

"Nice Greek girls are supposed to do three things in life," Vardalos says in an opening narration. "Marry Greek boys, make Greek babies and feed everyone until the day we die."

The film's bittersweet humor shines an affectionate light on smothering family love, generational battles and petty in-fighting, all of which have a universal quality."I have 27 first cousins," Vardalos tells her beau, played by John Corbett, after he tells her he comes from a small family. "My whole family is big and loud. And everybody is in each other's lives and business. All the time!"

2002
My Big Fat Greek Wedding

Directed by JOEL ZWICK

Starring: NIA VARDALOS (Toula Portokalos)   JOHN CORBETT (Ian Miller)
MICHAEL CONSTANTINE / LAINIE KAZAN / IAN GOMEZ

THE INTELLECTUAL JOHN CORBETT AND RESTAURANT WORKER NIA VARDALOS ARE TWO PEOPLE FROM THE SAME CHICAGO NEIGHBORHOOD LIVING VERY SEPARATE LIVES WHEN LOVE BRING THEM TOGETHER, DESPITE THEIR DIFFERENT BACKGROUNDS.

As Vardalos and Corbett bond (he's a handsome long-haired teacher), they seem headed for the wedding altar, though she has passing doubts. Then her mother, portrayed by Lainie Kazan, tells her it's time to call it off.

"Okay Toula, maybe you are having a little romance, hmm?" Mom says. "But end it now." Vardalos replies in a whisper "I love him," trying not to be defiant.

"My Big Fat Greek Wedding" has a few such moments of heavy drama, but mostly comedy reigns. The only thing exasperated Mom can say is, "Oh Toula, eat something, please," again underscoring that chowing down is central to Greek happiness. The comedy continues as Dad invites a succession of available Greek men—none of them with any charm—for dinner, trying to stoke a romance with Vardalos.

Corbett works hard at making himself an acceptable addition to the Greek family. When Corbett delivers some rehearsed Greek words, Vardalos' father, portrayed by Michael Constantine, is not impressed, muttering in Greek "When my people were writing philosophy, your people were still swinging from trees." This is translated for the audience as an English-language subtitle, but Vardalos tells the unaware Corbett this bald-faced lie, "He likes you!"

1. For a church wedding that will be a large and ornate affair, a retinue of bridesmaids prepare behind the scenes as their big moment draws near.

▲ 2

2. In the limousine after exchanging vows at the wedding altar, Nia Vardalos still can't believe she's married, especially since her character was drifting into middle age without any romance. New husband John Corbett isn't Greek like the rest of her chauvinistic family, but he makes an effort to fit in.

The wedding does justice to the film's title, with a mob of Greek relatives, women fussing around the bride behind the scenes, rituals in a Greek Orthodox Church that perplex Corbett's side of the aisle, and guests reveling in the post-ceremony reception.

The PG-rated film's budget is modest in large part due to its no-name cast, though they deliver exuberant and warm performances. Vardalos was nominated for an Oscar for original screenplay, which is based on her one-person stage play that caught Hollywood's attention.

But "My Big Fat Greek Wedding" became a big winner in the audience response category. The 1 hour, 35 minute movie, which was distributed to theaters by IFC Films, achieved an astronomical $241 million in North American box office sales and $369 million from cinemas worldwide.

Jack Nicholson and Diane Keaton seem to be portraying their real life personas in "Something's Gotta Give." Nicholson is a rich, 60-something man obsessed with bedding young woman, and the slightly-younger Keaton is an aloof but intellectually brilliant playwright.

"I have never lied to you," notorious playboy Nicholson tells Keaton in one climatic scene. "I have always told you some version of the truth." Not to let Nicholson wiggle out of accountability, Keaton shoots back, "The truth doesn't have versions, okay?" Keaton throws back Nicholson's exact words more literally later in the film, which reflects one of "Something's Gotta Give's" strengths.

"Something's Gotta Give" sports a solid supporting cast of Amanda Peet, Keanu Reeves, Oscar-winner Frances McDormand, John Favreau and Paul Michael Glaser. However, all except Peet are of little consequence with minor screen time, despite the film's longish 2 hours 8 minutes running time.

That's because Nicholson and Keaton are always at center stage, which is not surprising given that the pair has received four Oscars for acting from 16 nominations (including Keaton's nomination for "Something's Gotta Give"). The film is tailored for these two towering figures by writer and director Nancy Meyers, whose credits include the hit romantic comedies "It's Complicated" and "What Women Want."

The female characters have substance and are self empowered. "So is your play about us?" Nicholson frets when confronting Keaton after their romance peters out. "I'm going to be the laughing stock of Broadway?...Why is it you broads want all or nothing?" when it comes to romance. Responds Keaton in an assertive feminine retort, "We're just goofy when it comes to love."

2003
Something's Gotta Give

Directed by NANCY MEYERS

Starring: JACK NICHOLSON (Harry Sanborn)   DIANE KEATON (Erica Jane Barry)
KEANU REEVES / FRANCES MCDORMAND

Music by HANS ZIMMER

DIANE KEATON AND JACK NICHOLSON WARM UP TO EACH OTHER AT AN ELEGANT DINNER IN A TENDER MOMENT, BUT IT WAS A LONG ROAD TO TOGETHERNESS. THEY CLASHED WHEN THEY FIRST MET BECAUSE OF THEIR CONTRASTING PERSONALITIES. HE'S AN OLD MAN OBSESSED WITH DATING PRETTY YOUNG WOMAN, WHILE SHE'S AN INTELLECTUAL WOMAN NEARLY HIS AGE WHO IS NOT IMPRESSED WITH HIS TRENDY HIP HOP MUSIC BACKGROUND.

"The over-50 dating scene is geared towards men leaving older women out," McDormand says in a slice of Meyer's perceptive dialog. "And as a result, the women become more and more productive and therefore, more and more interesting. Which, in turn, makes them even less desirable because as we all know men, especially older men, are threatened and deathly afraid of productive and interesting women."

The 2003 release by Columbia Pictures in the U.S. can be viewed as a modern version of the 1930s mad-cap romantic comedy genre, whose formula mixes genuine romance with occasional contrivances that jack up a plot's amusement quotient. Among the updates are Viagra jokes and emotional exchanges via instant email messaging that is a proxy for conversation. Nicholson carries on as an irrepressible dirty-old-man, even

1

And perhaps the biggest contrivance is that audiences get convinced that the cultured Keaton character falls in love with a cradle-robbing Lothario like Nicholson, moments after he quits dating Keaton's own daughter Peet.

When Keaton confronts Nicholson for his slovenly behavior while he's her house guest recovering from a heart attack, the irrepressible bachelor has to cut short a phone call with "Can I call you right back doll?" to one of his bimbo girlfriends. Then Nicholson turns to Keaton saying innocently "Hey, what's up?" But the movie works because audiences see in Nicholson the charming womanizer who women know they should avoid like the plague, but still can't seem to resist.

1. Striking a familiar pose, Jack Nicholson is flat on back as the nubile and much-younger Amanda Peet snuggles him from on top. Jack's character likes to date women young enough to be his grand-daughter, until Peet's sophisticated mother catches his eye.

2. Diane Keaton's love life gets complicated when a handsome young doctor, portrayed by Keanu Reeves starts to woo her. This sets up a love triangle since Jack Nicholson is also vying for her heart.

«- Julian:
And when something happens to you that's
never happened to you before, don't you have
to find out what it is?-»

1 ▲

2 ▶

«-Harry: I have never lied to you.
I have always told you some
version of the truth. -»

1. Diane Keaton has to prop up a woozy Jack Nicholson, after he is rushed to the hospital with mild chest pains. He's something of a dirty old man who tries to get frisky in his hospital gown.

2. After a brief stay at a local hospital, Jack Nicholson takes his doctor's advice of getting rest. So he makes himself at home as an unexpected guest at the nearby beach home of Diane Keaton.

True love is supposed to be eternal, but for Drew Barrymore in "50 First Dates", it evaporates every day with the regularity of an alarm clock. As a result of a car accident, her character is afflicted with a brain disorder that erases the prior day's events from her mind, though she retains her pre-accident memories.

The trouble is that her love interest, Adam Sandler entered her life after her accident, meaning he's a regular casualty of her short-term memory loss. "Nothing beats a first kiss," Barrymore says in a montage sequence showing how Sandler must repeatedly court her. "That's what I've heard," responds a Sandler in a bittersweet moment.

The setting for this stop-start romance is Hawaii, which provides lush tropical backdrops and picturesque beaches for the movie, which was released in 2004 by Columbia Pictures. The supporting cast is also noteworthy, and includes youth comedy star Rob Schneider, Sean Astin ("Lord of the Rings") and comedy legend Dan Akroyd.

The Sandler character is a marine biologist who in his free time prowls the island's tourist bars romancing a succession of vacationing women. Relationships are always short-term affairs because the women are just passing through, which is fine for the commitment-phobic Sandler. But he then succumbs to the voluptuous and free-spirited Barrymore, whose character is a local resident— and thus won't be jetting back to the mainland anytime soon.

At first, Sandler runs into resistance from Barrymore's protective family, but his persistence and sincerity wins them over. When a memory-challenged Barrymore snaps at Sandler, "don't call me Lucy [her character's name]. I barely know you," her father gently corrects her saying, "Sweetie, you are sort of dating him." This leaves Barrymore wide-eyed and slack-jawed. The dough-faced Sandler, with his everyman looks, tries to be reassuring to his perplexed love with a self-deprecating joke, "Sorry I'm not better looking."

Barrymore's amnesia provides plenty of other plot turns that are comic, tragic or sometimes both. On one occasion, Barrymore throws a fit when she doesn't recognize Sandler, and then pursues him afterwards with an apologetic, "I was so nervous to come here to meet the guy who makes me fall in love with him every day."

2004
50 First Dates

Directed by PETER SEGAL

Starring: ADAM SANDLER (Henry Roth)   DREW BARRYMORE (Lucy Whitmore)
ROB SCHNEIDER / SEAN ASTIN / DAN AYKROYD

Music by TEDDY CASTELLUCCI

BUBBLY AND BEAUTIFUL DREW BARRYMORE LEADS AN IDYLLIC LIFE WITH HER FAMILY IN TROPICAL HAWAII, EXCEPT THERE'S ONE PROBLEM. DUE TO AN ACCIDENT, SHE LOSES HER SHORT-TERM MEMORY WHEN SLEEPING, SO SHE DOESN'T REMEMBER THE NEW MAN IN HER LIFE THE NEXT MORNING. SHE MAKES AN PERMANENT IMPRESSION ON A MARINE BIOLOGIST, ADAM SANDLER, WHEN HE SEES HER FREQUENTLY HAVING BREAKFAST ALONE AT THE LOCAL DINER, BUT HER MEMORY LAPS-ES FORCE SANDLER TO CONCOCT INGENIOUS SCHEMES IN THE HUMOROUS COURTSHIP THAT FOLLOWS.

Because Sandler's character works with animals, the movie works in scenes of a captive walrus, a penguin and other exotic marine creatures in Sandler's care. His rapport is such that the animals seem to understand and respond to his conversation, which audiences can view as either charming or absurd.

In another diversion, "'50 First Dates' is loaded with crude toilet humor to appeal to Sandler's traditional teen male audience, which he is grad-ually outgrowing in this film. Characters joke about breasts, condoms, wet dreams, pimping and penises. When in his bar hopping mode, Sandler promotes the prospect of "guilt-free vigorous sex with me" to a pretty blonde vacationer.

But on tender track separate from that coarse humor, the movie presents a sentimental love story where it's apparent that Barrymore does retain a permanent recollection of Sandler despite her repetitive amnesia lapses. Her love for Sandler is the only thing that breaches her memo-ry barrier.

Film critics give Sandler and Barrymore high praise for projecting on-screen chemistry in their romance. They had practice, because they were also paired in the 1998 romantic comedy "The Wedding Singer."

"A Very Long Engagement" ("Un long dimanche de fiançailles") guides audiences on an engrossing journey using intricate flashbacks that present a tragic and hauntingly romantic mystery.

In the 2004 French-language film (with English subtitles), there's the puppy love of a young couple, the horrors of World War I suffered by the young man, portrayed by Gaspard Ulliel, and a post-war mystery. Leading French actress Audrey Tautou plays a young woman searching for her love Ulliel after WWI ends, despite his being listed as killed in action.

"If (he) were dead, (Tautou) would know," narration by Florence Thomassin tells the audience. "Since the death notice, she stubbornly holds on to her intuition, like to a flimsy wire. She never gets discouraged."

While a serious drama, "A Very Long Engagement" is also full of sly irony and bits of humor that make the audience chuckle in places. The movie is based on a best-selling French novel published in 1991. And like most French films, it presents an earthy view of the human condition. In fleeting moments, it presents a discreet discussion of masturbation, bordello scenes and short bursts of undressed sex, which contribute to a restrictive R audience classification for its U.S release.

The 2 hour, 13 minute film is also unblinking in its lengthy portrayal of the bloody horrors of the First World War, which may strike some as out of place in a love story. But those horrors were seared into a generation that came to believe that God died on the Western European battlefields in the senseless carnage of trench warfare and open-field assaults against machine guns.

"I hear her heart beating, like Morse code," the baby-faced, 19-year-old Ulliel tells a sympathetic guard in a flashback scene during WWI. "We're engaged. Luckily...now I can go straight home after (my) execution." Ulliel has been convicted by the French army for injuring himself intentionally to get medical leave. Although he has clearly lost his sanity, he is being sent on a suicide mission to serve as a decoy in No Man's Land to rouse German gunners.

2004

A Very Long Engagement

Directed by JEAN-PIERRE JEUNET

Starring: AUDREY TAUTOU (Mathilde Donnay)   GASPARD ULLIEL (Manech Langonnet)
MARION COTILLARD / ANDRÉ DUSSOLLIER / JODIE FOSTER

Music by ANGELO BADALAMENTI

WORLD WAR I IS OVER AND HER LOVE IS PRESUMED KILLED, LEAVING AUDREY TAUTOU ALONE WITH JUST HER MEMORIES ON TOP OF A COASTAL LIGHTHOUSE THAT WAS A TOUCHSTONE FOR THEIR ROMANCE BEFORE THE WAR.

▲ 1

1. and 2. Gaspard Ulliel portrays a young soldier never seen again after being con-
demned to serve as a decoy in World War I's No Man's Land—the killing zone
between opposing lines. After the war, his pre-war lover relentlessly pursues
clues on his fate.

2 ▲

After the war, Tautou doggedly tracks down soldiers who were on the scene and pursues other leads on the faint hope Ulliel did not die. After three years of searching, her family pleads she's being unreasonable, but she responds firmly, "No, I call that hope."

Two-time Oscar winner Jodie Foster fills a French-speaking supporting role as the widow of one of Ulliel's army comrades. Director Jean-Pierre Jeunet also has an Oscar pedigree. He was nominated for co-writing the French blockbuster "Amelie", the 2001 whimsical comedy also starring Tautou.

The $55 million film production, a sky-high price tag by French standards, faithfully recreated WWI battlefields and Paris in the 1920s for unparalleled atmospherics. "A Very Long Engagement" was nominated for two Oscars, in Best Cinematography and Best Art Direction, categories where most of the competition was from Hollywood films.

«- MATHILDE (TAUTOU): MIRACLES DON'T JUST HAPPEN IN LOURDES, YOU KNOW. »

The screen is filled with sweeping views of a coastal lighthouse that's a touchstone for Tautou, aerial views including majestic steam locomotives gliding across the countryside, and gripping WWI battlefields. The atmospherics also include slightly washed out colors and a frequent dark hue that gives the audience a feeling of peering through the mists of time.

While those cinema visuals were widely praised, some were taken aback by the juxtaposition of a love story intertwined with WWI inhumanity. Reflecting mixed reaction, the French government nominated another film as the country's official Oscar entry for foreign film for 2004.

However, "A Very Long Engagement" won five Cesar Awards (France's equivalent to the Oscars) and received seven other Cesar nominations. Elsewhere, "A Very Long Engagement" was nominated as one of the best foreign-language films by Britain's top cinema organization and Hollywood's Golden Globes.

A tramp steamer is a speck in the open ocean as it sails to an uncharted island on a mysterious expedition financed by a reckless moviemaker.

This is high adventure circa 1930s in the 2005 version of "King Kong," which is a remake of the 1933 black & white classic. The newer version methodically zigzags between comedy, bubbling adventure, romance and deadly drama over its lengthy 3 hour, 7 minute running time, during which viewers are left on the edge of their seats by numerous cliff-hangers.

"King Kong" opens with comedic touches in Depression-era New York City and then transitions to sheer adventure, as experienced by Naomi Watts, who portrays a beautiful neophyte actress hired to sail to a location shoot.

The ship's captain asks Watts if she's nervous as they embark on the voyage, to which she replies, "Nervous. No, why? Should I be?" The captain, portrayed by German actor Thomas Kretschmann, who looks like a macho U Boat skipper complete with a Teutonic accent, adds softly with a touch of foreboding, "It isn't every woman who would take such risk."

Watts, Adrien Brody and Jack Black carry the PG-13 rated film. Rotund comedic actor Black is an irrepressible film producer who is a lovable rogue.

"I'm somebody you can trust, Ann," Black says earnestly to Watts when recruiting her. "I'm a movie producer." That's not too long after the audience hears Black tell a subordinate in another scene, "All you had to do is look her in the eye and lie," in one of many dashes of humor mocking Tinseltown.

"King Kong" is also an improbably complicated romance. On the cruise to the mysterious Skull Island, the movie's screen-writer—portrayed by previous Oscar winner Brody—starts a budding romance with Watts.

Island natives snatch Watts and serve her up as a live sacrifice to the giant special-effects creation that is King Kong, who becomes intrigued with his little blonde-haired bauble. Later, the giant ape rescues Watts from being devoured in the jungle and that leaves Watts to run after the chest-thumping, roaring King Kong for protection. "Wait!" shouts Watts, which prompts King Kong to put her on his shoulder as he strides through the jungle.

2005
King Kong

Directed by PETER JACKSON

Starring: NAOMI WATTS (Ann Darrow)   ADRIEN BRODY (Jack Driscoll)
JACK BLACK / THOMAS KRETSCHMANN / COLIN HANKS / JAMIE BELL

Music by JAMES NEWTON HOWARD

FRAMED BY NEW YORK CITY'S URBAN LANDSCAPE CIRCA 1930S, KING KONG GENTLY HOLDS NAOMI WATTS ATOP EMPIRE STATE BUILDING, AFTER HE ESCAPES A STAGE SHOW WHERE HE WAS ON DISPLAY. BELOW, THE MILITARY IS PREPARING AN ASSAULT ON THE GIANT APE.

2

▲ 1

An unspoken, cross-species emotional bond with King Kong has Watts conflicted when she is rescued by Brody, who sneaks her away from the ape's lair. In pursuing Watts, King Kong is subdued and transported to New York for a carnival-like display that breaks the heart of Watts and sets the stage for the final act of "going ape" in the streets of New York.

"Wait, no!" shrieks Watts as her human rescuers push her into a row boat to leave the island as they are pursued by King Kong. "It's me he wants. Please stop this!" shouts Watts, distraught she can't prevent the men from brutally capturing King Kong. Audiences can conclude the big ape is driven even wilder at seeing Watts handled roughly by her male companions as he pursues them.

The special effects-laden extravaganza won three Oscars in technical categories—sound editing, sound mixing and visual effects. "King Kong" was also nominated for an Academy Award in art direction. Special effects for the island jungle are particularly arresting with realistic huge insects, bloodthirsty dinosaurs pursuing Watts at every turn and, of course, King Kong atop a strange and amazing ecosystem then unknown to the outside world.

1. A rescue party braves the creatures and geographic hazards of Skull Island but pays a heavy price as they battle bizarre jungle animals both big and small. The natural beauty of the island hides many dangers.

2. King Kong frequently lets out a fearsome roar. Behind his loud bluster, the giant ape seems to have a soft side, but it is suppressed by a constant need to fend off attacking animals and humans.

To conjure up the screen magic for "King Kong," Universal Pictures commissioned New Zealander Peter Jackson as director and co-writer after his triumph as the Oscar-winning creative force behind the epic "The Lord of the Rings" cinema trilogy.

Jackson's 2005 film is a true homage to the 1933 original (Hollywood also generated a 1976 remake). The Jackson epic follows the same basic storyline down to the tragic and signature climax of King Kong cornered atop the Empire State Building, taken down by a hail of bullets from military bi-planes.

1. and 2. King Kong becomes obsessed with the comparatively slight Naomi Watts. It's not quite clear what the attraction is but she's female from a somewhat related species and certainly different from what King Kong sees in his jungle habitat.

... Oh, no, it wasn't the airplanes. Twas Beauty killed the Beast.

"Mamma Mia!" is what Hollywood calls a "chick flick." The musical romantic comedy appeals to a female audience, which can identify with three middle-aged women—played by Meryl Streep, Christine Baranski and Julie Waters—who energetically belt out songs, enjoy an unguarded camaraderie and display a lusty self-confidence.

The 2008 Universal Pictures release was a cinema adaptation of a long-running hit stage musical that, in turn, was inspired by and is peppered with chart-topping songs from ABBA. That's the Swedish pop music band with a succession of English-language hits from the 1970s and 1980s including the bouncy "Dancing Queen," "SOS," "Waterloo" and the eponymous title tune. The actors vocalized those familiar ABBA tunes—17 of them in the movie—and their performances were surprisingly good for the most part, despite their not being professional singers.

The movie's improbable story starts with single-mother Streep organizing a wedding for her daughter, portrayed by pretty blonde Amanda Seyfried on the Greek island where they operate a tourist hotel. That setting provides breezy Mediterranean patios, hilltop seascape vistas ripe for romance, and a succession of European characters.

After stumbling upon her mother's old diary, the adventurous Seyfried secretly invites three long-lost loves of her mother, one of which she suspects is her father. "I feel like there's a part of me missing," she confides to two friends of her plot. "And when I meet my Dad, everything will fall into place."

When the three middle-age fatherly prospects arrive—Pierce Brosnan, Colin Firth and Stellan Skarsgård—the bride only gets more confused, and her surprised mother Streep bursts into an emotional and musical tizzy. Uncertainty about the father of the bride interrupts the ceremony, which takes an unexpected turn of events when wedding vows are finally exchanged.

2008
Mamma Mia !

Directed by PHYLLIDA LLOYD

Starring: MERYL STREEP (Donna Sheridan) PIERCE BROSNAN (Sam Carmichael)
AMANDA SEYFRIED / COLIN FIRTH / STELLAN SKARSGÅRD / JULIE WALTERS / CHRISTINE BARANSKI

Music by STIG ANDERSON / BENNY ANDERSSON / BJÖRN ULVAEUS

MERYL STREEP AND PIERCE BROSNAN PONDER WHETHER HE IS THE FATHER OF HER DAUGHTER
FROM A SHORT ROMANCE MANY YEARS AGO, AND IF ANY ROMANTIC FLAME REMAINS.

« -Sam Carmichael:
   I'm a divorced man who's loved you for 21 years.-»

▲ 1

1. Meryl Streep bounces off a bed like it's a trampoline, encouraged by two women friends from her youth (pictured at sides) who are visiting, as well as by three men who romanced her at different times, and who all show up again prior to her daughter's wedding.

2. Meryl Streep shakes off the doldrums of middle age as she slides down a stairway banister, energized that her daughter is about to get married.

As the story unfolds, the unmarried Streep professes to have no interest in igniting new sparks with any of her three old flames. Instead, she reverts to her carefree youth with two longtime female friends who arrive as guests for the wedding.

Their personal girl talk rambles over their memories of old times, breast implants, money and the infirmities of old age. Wealthy divorcée Baranski moans to her friends, "Help me out of these boots. All that freakin' yoga has made my feet bigger."

Of course, the girl talk eventually meanders to the current state of their love lives, to which Streep protests, "It takes too much energy. Oh god, I'm just so glad that whole part of my life is over, you know. Seriously!" Of course, her resolve gets tested by the wine, sun and past romantic flames.

Traditional musicals have fallen out of favor with Hollywood audiences over the decades, but "Mamma Mia!" became a cinema exception as the year's fifth ranked film, grossing $610 million at theaters around the world. That shattered a 30-year-old box office record for top musical film held by John Travolta's song-fest "Grease."

1. Meryl Streep (left) beams with pride as she accompanies her daughter portrayed by Amanda Seyfried as she is about to wed on the Greek island where they live. Two bridesmaids follow in the background to the right.

2. A wedding on a Greek island in the Mediterranean fires up the wedding party and sets the stage for a ceremony where the bride and groom are a surprise to those on hand.

A 17-year-old girl finds that her personal life changes along with the weather when she moves from sunny Arizona to the rainy and gloomy Pacific coast of Washington state. After an unhappy arrival at her new high school, her spirits pick up when she is smitten by a stand-offish teenage boy from an insular and odd family.

That's the storyline of "Twilight," the 2008 supernatural romantic drama that launched the blockbuster movie series. But the movie is more complex as Kristen Stewart, who portrays the transplanted girl, becomes increasingly disaffected by well-meaning gestures of those around her, pushing her into the arms of mysterious new classmate Robert Pattinson.

"What if I'm not the hero," Pattinson tells Stewart, trying to warn her off. "What if I'm the bad guy?...It would be better if we weren't friends, not that I don't want to be."

After digesting various cues, Stewart realizes Pattinson and his family are vampires, but non-threatening because they live off animals and not human blood. That supernatural storyline provides plenty of opportunities for melodrama—both gentle and sinister.

Over a quiet dinner in a restaurant, Pattinson struggles to admit, "I don't have the strength to stay away from you anymore." Stewart then replies softly, "Then don't."

Stewart's sleepy Pacific Northwest town is jolted by a series of bloody murders, at first thought to have been committed by an animal, until human tracks are found. Her character eventually becomes at risk.

As events unfold, Stewart's thoughts about Pattinson are expressed in a voiceover: "There was a part of him, and I didn't know how dominant that part might be, that thirsted for my blood. (But) I was unconditionally and irrevocably in love with him."

The attraction for "Twilight's" rabid teenagers is the tragedy of love that cannot be consummated, because the lad is a vampire and thus an immortal that won't age. There is also a romantic tension as Stewart surrenders herself to Pattinson, relying on him for her safety.

The well-crafted film deftly presents a succession of stark contrasts. The pale white faces of Pattinson's vampire family and Stewart jump out at the audience from the grey backdrops of the Pacific Northwest. Those faces are further highlighted by dark eyebrows and black hair, and the vampires' reddish lips. These characters often wear brooding, unhappy looks on their faces, making them look even further apart from others around them.

2008
Twilight

Directed by CATHERINE HARDWICKE

Starring: KRISTEN STEWART (Bella Swan) ROBERT PATTINSON (Edward Cullen)
PETER FACINELLI / ELIZABETH REASER / BILLY BURKE

Music by CARTER BURWELL

AT HER NEW HIGH SCHOOL, KRISTEN STEWART BECOMES ATTRACTED TO ROBERT PATTINSON, A HANDSOME TEENAGER WHO IS BROODING AND ANTI-SOCIAL. SHE FEELS SOMETHING UNSEEN IS STANDING BETWEEN THEM.

▲ 1

1. Lonely high school girl Kirsten Stewart learns why the laws of physics don't seem to apply to classmate Robert Pattinson. Though he tries to conceal it, he can climb heights like tall trees in an instant and move in bursts of speed that the human eye can barely follow.

2. Does he want to kiss her or devour her? It's not really clear what's in Robert Pattinson heart as he eyes Kristen Stewart while they dance.

In another contrast, some scenes play out in slow motion while in others, the vampires move with superhuman speed. The forests of the Pacific Northwest complete the package with murky shadows that in some places are fractured by shafts of light from the sun peaking through omnipresent clouds. Those woods also conceal shadowy figures that are a menace to unlucky and careless humans who are caught alone.

Oscar voters judged the PG 13 film as merely a teenage melodrama and passed over the 2-hour-long movie for awards.

But "Twilight" is noteworthy for having women in the two most important behind-the-camera posts that in most other films are occupied by males. The director is Catherine Hardwicke and the co-screenwriter is Melissa Rosenberg—which is fitting for a film crafted to appeal to a primarily female audience. In addition, the movie is based on a best-selling novel series authored by Stephenie Meyer.

The success of the 2008 original shocked Hollywood, since the film incarnation had long languished unmade. Then-unheralded independent distributor Summit Entertainment stepped forward to make "Twilight" for $37 million. Though that is about half the cost average of a major studio film at the time, the film was a gamble because of its cast of largely unknown actors. But with the fan base from the novel and a movie that turned out to be very entertaining, "Twilight" rolled up a blockbuster $385 million in global box offices, spawning additional films.

« –Edward: You don't know how long I've waited for you. »

Coco Chanel is most famous for building the fashion empire that bears her name, but history also remembers her as an early feminist. Her sleek and elegant fashions liberated women from ornamental flowers, feathers and other excesses from the ladies fashions of her youth.

In the 2009 French-language movie "Coco Before Chanel" ("Coco avant Chanel"), Audrey Tautou portrays the fashion icon in her rise from poverty and early years of love, lust and feminine liberation.

"I always knew I'd be no one's wife," Tautou tells the love of her life Alessandro Nivola, as he stands silently next to her. She then turns to him and adds in a whisper of a voice, "Not even yours. It's just sometimes, I forget."

Nivola portrays a charming British businessman who intends to marry another woman for her money, even though he is smitten with Tautou. Given her own mercenary motives for love in the past, Tautou is in no position to moralize about his choice.

Like the other characters in "Coco Before Chanel," he's a real-life person from the fashion designer's life—Arthur Capel, who everyone called "Boy Capel" from his childhood nickname.

Raised in an orphanage and poor as a young woman, Tautou's character makes her way in the world by attaching herself to wealthy men, notably Nivola and a rich French aristocrat played by Benoît Poelvoorde. It is the idle rich and avuncular Poelvoorde who takes Tautou into his baronial estate, bed and high society.

Tautou comes across as something of a modern-day courtesan—a woman who is kept as a mistress in court society by one aristocrat or another. In the bedroom, her interludes with Poelvoorde lack romance or love, but then his business associate Nivola enters her life.

"Ever been in love?" Tautou asks another woman, since she is inexperienced and cynical about romance based on her experiences with men. The response does not encourage when Tautou is told, "It never made me happy. It hurts."

2009
Coco Before Chanel

Directed by ANNE FONTAINE

Starring: AUDREY TAUTOU (Gabrielle "Coco" Chanel) ALESSANDRO NIVOLA (Arthur Capel)
BENOÎT POELVOORDE / EMMANUELLE DEVOS / MARIE GILLAIN

Music by ALEXANDRE DESPLAT

AUDREY TAUTOU HAS ONE GENUINE LOVE IN HER TROUBLED LIFE—A BRITISH BUSINESSMAN PORTRAYED BY ALESSANDRO NIVOLA. THEY ARE SWEPT UP IN ROMANCE, CAN HE REALLY MAKE A LIFE-LONG COMMITMENT?

The movie does not attempt to make the Tautou character warm or likeable. Coco Chanel is portrayed as aloof and a little bitter, but it's re-alistic because audiences learn that she was abandoned as a child and later was unable to make a decent living as a saloon singer.

When Poelvoorde asks her to reconsider when she says she is leaving, Tautou reminds, "My moodiness tires you."

But the relationship between the older Poelvoorde and Tautou is complex. At first, Tautou appears to be just another sweet, young thing passing through the bacchanalian life of the idle wealthy, including occasional wild parties. But when the torn Nivola seems poised to sweep Tautou away, Poelvoorde cautions, "I don't want you to leave. I'm afraid. Afraid you'll be unhappy. Afraid you'll suddenly lose everything."

▲ 1

«-The only interesting thing about love is making love –
too bad you need a guy for that.-» **Coco Chanel**

1. Audrey Tautou portrays fabled designer Coco Chanel working in her own fashion studio after gaining the success that came from her simple but elegant designs—a sharp break with the flowery fashions of her youth.

2. The cultured and affable Alessandro Nivola—who is a French-speaking English businessman—opened the doors of French high society to the founder of the Chanel fashion empire early in her life.

Some critics say that the fashion icon depicted in "Coco Before Chanel" is so chilly, it's not clear why men would be attracted to her. But Tautou has a pixie cuteness, and Chanel's early fashion sets her apart from other women and her intelligence is magnetic.

While a thoroughly French film, "Coco Before Chanel" is a co-production that includes Warner Bros. Entertainment France—which is part of the Hollywood major studio. Sony Pictures Classics distributed in the U.S.

The 1 hour, 50 minute movie is rated a mildly restrictive PG-13 for some scenes showing the start of passionate love making—but no nudity—and also lovers quarreling in the bedroom. "Coco Before Chanel" received one Oscar nomination Best Costume Design, which should be no surprise, since the origin of 20th century couture is weaved into the fabric of the film.

Wearing simple but stylish outfits, Tautou sniffs at the feathers, ruffles and heavy jewelry of her contemporaries. "She likes dresses with no corsets, shoes with no heels, hats with no feathers," Poelvoorde marvels at one point. "That's my Coco."

« -Étienne Balsan and Coco Chanel:
I couldn't guess your age.
How old? 16? 25?
When I'm bored I feel ancient.
And how old do you feel now?
A thousand years.-»

The founder of the Chanel couture dynasty portrayed by Audrey Tautou places herself in eyecatching settings, such as this mirrored staircase.

The jungle on the planet Pandora is a lush blue and the bright flora looks inviting, but things aren't what they seem. Hidden in the jungle are creatures and plants that are killers, but the world of "Avatar" is also where two inter-locked characters, both portrayed by Sam Worthington, find love via a cross-species romance.

In the 2009 film "Avatar," Worthington is a handsome young military man who has lost the use of his legs. But he gets liberated when he is connected to a second body that is an avatar—a separate body that in this case, was created by scientists. It's the year 2154 and Earthlings have created avatar proxies in the image of the indigenous Na'vi humanoids. The avatars don't need breathing masks like humans do on Pandora.

The Na'vi are tall, slender blue humanoids with yellow eyes. With lithe slinky bodies, they have a sexy quality. Worthington's avatar becomes romantically involved with a Na'vi voiced by Zoe Saldana, whose character is feminine and yet with the fighting skills of a male soldier.

"You have a strong heart (and) no fear," Saldana's character Neytiri tells Worthington, after she rescues his blundering avatar named Jake from being killed by jungle creatures. "But stupid. Ignorant like a child."

She teaches Worthington's avatar how to survive the perils of Pandora and the avatar gets inducted in Neytiri's tribe, which has a sophisticated culture that leads a low-tech life in close harmony with nature.

They eventually marry in the Na'vi tradition, which isn't depicted as particularly sensual, in order to keep "Avatar's" audience classification PG-13 for theatrical release. "I am with you now, Jake," Neytiri tells him. "We are mated for life...It is our way."

Audiences can associate this and other elements of "Avatar" with concepts that are familiar to Earth. The mating brings to mind Eskimos who rub noses to kiss. And the Na'vi are like American Indians, in that both are depicted as abused by the culture with superior technology. Indeed, the leader of the Na'vi tribe is voiced by Native American actor Wes Studi, whose acting credits include a role in the revisionist American Western "Dances with Wolves."

SAM WORTHINGTON'S AVATAR (LEFT)—A SATELLITE BODY THAT IS SCIENTIFICALLY ENGINEERED TO MATCH THE HUMANOID NAVI SPECIES ON THE PLANET PANDORA—TAKES A BOW-AND-ARROW LESSON FROM A NA'VI FEMALE PORTRAYED BY ZOE SALDANA. HIS AVATAR IS EVENTUALLY ACCEPTED TO JOIN HER TRIBE.

2009
Avatar

Directed by JAMES CAMERON

Starring: SAM WORTHINGTON (Jake Sully) ZOE SALDANA (Neytiri)
SIGOURNEY WEAVER / GIOVANNI RIBISI / MICHELLE RODRÍGUEZ

Music by JAMES HORNER

(306) 04-03   View   Select   Object   Object Mode   Global

50   100   150   200   250   300   350   400   450

Sam Worthington's avatar is caught in the middle of a looming war between visiting humans and the native Na'vi population that includes Neytiri (right), portrayed by Zoe Saldana. Worthington's Na'vi avatar is controlled by his human body that is paraplegic from injuries.

50   100   150   200   250   300   350   400   450

A

Aajkovskij, Petr, Il'ia, 110
ABBA, 264
Adair, Tom, 110
Adamson, Andrew, 234
Affair to Remember, An, 13, 108, 109, 202, 204
Affleck, Ben, 228
African Queen, The, 66, 69
Aiello, Danny, 178
Aimee, Anouk, 134, 135, 135c
Airplane!, 184
Aladdin, 198, 199
Albert, Eddie, 80, 82, 85c
Albertson, Mabel, 136
Alexander, Jason, 188, 193
Alice in Wonderland, 114
Allen, Woody, 152, 153, 153c, 154, 155c
Amadeus, 220
Amelie, 255
American Film Institute, 22
America's sweetheart, 183
Anderson, Benny, 264
Anderson, Stig, 264
Andrews, Julie, 128
Andrews, Naveen, 218
Anna Karenina, 30, 35
Annie Hall, 13, 22, 152, 154, 232
Armstrong, Louis, 100, 102, 105c
Ashman, Howard, 194, 198
Astin, Sean, 250
Auric, Georges, 80
Avatar, 12, 227, 280, 281
Aykroyd, 250

B

Back to the Future, 168
Badalamenti, Angelo, 252
Balaban, Barney, 91
Bananas, 152
Baranski, Christine, 264, 267
Barefoot in the Park, 13, 136, 138
Barouh, Pierre, 134
Barry, John, 162
Barrymore, Drew, 250, 251, 251c
Bartholomew, Freddie, 30
Bates, Kathy, 222
Beatty, Warren, 140, 140c, 141
Beauty and the Beast, 10, 11, 12, 194, 196
Bedard, Irene, 212
Bell, Jamie, 258
Bellamy, Ralph, 188, 193
Benson, Robby, 194, 196
Bergman, Ingrid, 50, 50c, 52c, 53, 54c
Bicycle Thief, The, 122
Binoche, Juliette, 218, 219
Black, Jack, 258
Blixen, Karen, 168
Blount, Lisa, 160
Bogart, Humphrey, 11, 50, 50c, 52c, 53, 54c, 66, 66c, 68, 69, 69c, 71, 71c, 86, 86c, 88, 91c, 93c
Bonham Carter, Helena, 170, 171c, 172, 173c
Bonnie and Clyde, 13, 140, 141
Bovasso, Julie, 178
Boyer, Charles, 136
Brandauer, Klaus, Maria, 162, 164, 165c
Brett, Jeremy, 124
Bridge on the River Kwai, 130
Bridges of Madison County, The, 11, 216, 217
Broderick, Matthew, 174, 175
Brody, Andrien, 258, 260
Brosnan, Pierce, 264, 265c
Brown Clarence, 30, 35
Bruns, Gorge, 110
Burke, Billy, 270
Burwell, Carter, 270
Bus Stop, 13, 15, 106, 107

C

50 First Dates, 250, 251
Cage, Nicolas, 178, 179, 179c
California Suite, 138
Callow, Simon, 172

Cameron, James, 11, 222, 225, 227, 280, 281
Cannes Film Festival, 135
Capel, Arthur, 274
Capra, Frank, 12, 24, 27
Casablanca, 13, 50
Cassel, Vincent, 234
Castellucci, Teddy, 250
Castle Rock Entertainment, 183
Chaplin, Charlie, 11, 14, 18, 18c, 21c, 22, 22c
Chaplin, Geraldine, 130
Chariots of Fire, 156
Cher, 178, 179, 179c
Cherrill, Virginia, 18
Chicago, 220
Chiles, Lois, 150
Christie, Julie, 14, 130c, 131, 133c
Cinderella, 56, 64, 114
City Lights, 11, 14, 18, 22
Claire, Ina, 18, 48
Clark, Les, 110
Clements, Ron, 198
Cocker, Joe, 204
Coco Before Chanel, 274, 277
Colbert, Claudette, 12, 24, 24c, 26c, 27, 27c, 29c
Coleman, Dabney, 156, 157
Columbia Pictures, 24, 151, 183, 245, 250
Connolly, Walter, 24
Constantine, Michael, 240, 241
Cooper, Gladys, 124
Corbett, John, 240, 241, 241c, 243, 243c
Cotillard, Marion, 252
Could Have Danced All Night, I, 128
Courtenay, Tom, 130
Crosby, Bing, 100, 100c, 102, 105c
Crying Game, 220
Crystal, Billy, 10, 180, 180c, 181, 183, 183c
Cukor, George, 124, 127
Curtiz, Michael, 50

D

Dafoe, Willem, 218
Dances with Wolves, 280
Dancing Queen, 264
Darling, 97
David, Mach, 56
Day-Lewis, Daniel, 170, 172
De Havilland, Olivia, 38, 40
Dench, Judi, 170, 172, 228, 230, 232, 232c
Denning, Richard, 108
Desplat, Alexandre, 274
Devos, Emmanuelle, 274
Dewhurst, Colleen, 154
Diaz, Cameron, 234, 237c
DiCaprio, Leonardo, 142, 222, 223c, 225, 225c, 226c
Die Hard 2: Die Harder, 186
Dillman, Bradford, 150, 151
Dinesen, Isak, 168
Dion, Celine, 204
Doctor Zhivago, 13, 14, 130, 131
Donner, Richard, 174, 177
Douglas, Melvyn, 48
Douglas, Mike, 63
DreamWorks, 236
Dukakis, Olympia, 178, 179
Dunaway, Faye, 140, 140c
Dussollier, Adré, 252
Duvall, Shelley, 154

E

Eastwood, Clint, 11, 216, 217, 217c
Ebert, Roger, 142
Edelman, Herbert, 136, 151
Elizondo, Hector, 188, 193c
Elliott, Denholm, 170, 172
Elsom, Isobel, 98
English Patient, The, 12, 218, 219, 220
Ephron, Nora, 202
E.T.-The Extra-Terrestrial, 210
Everett, Rupert, 228

F

Facinelli, Peter, 270
Farrow, Mia, 35
Favreau, John, 244
Feature Fil, 234
Field, Betty, 106
Fiennes, Joseph, 228, 229c, 230, 231c
Fiennes, Ralph, 218, 219, 219c, 220c
Firth, Colin, 218, 228, 232c, 264
Fisher, Carrie, 180
Fisher, Frances, 222
Fitzgerald, Barry, 72, 75c
Fleming, Victor, 38, 40
Fonda, Henry, 156, 157, 157c
Fonda, Jane, 136, 136c, 138, 139c, 156, 157
Fontaine, Anne, 274
Ford, John, 72, 73
Forester, E., M., 172
Forrest Gump, 232
Foster, Jodie, 252, 255
Freeman, Jonathan, 198
Friedhofer, Hugo, 108

G

Gable, Clark, 12, 24, 24c, 26c, 27, 27c, 29c, 38, 38c, 40, 40c, 42c, 44c
Gabriel, Mike, 212
Garbo, Greta, 11, 30, 30c, 32, 32c, 35, 35c, 36c, 48, 48c
Garden of the Finzi-Continis, The, 122
Gardenia, Vincent, 178
Gere, Richard, 160, 161, 161c, 188, 189c, 193, 193c
Geronimi, Clyde, 56, 94, 110
Gerson, Betty, Lou, 63
Get Me to the Church On Time, 128
Ghost, 184, 186
Gibson, Mel, 212, 213
Gillain, Marie, 274
Giuffrè, Aldo, 118
Glaser, Paul, Michael, 244
Godfather, The, 148, 178
Godfrey, Patrick, 170
Going My Way, 72
Goldberg, Eric, 212
Goldberg, Whoopi, 184, 186
Goldblum, Jeff, 152, 154
Golden Pond, On, 15, 156, 157
Goldwyn, Tony, 184
Gomez, Ian, 240
Goodbye Girl, The, 138
Gone with the Wind, 12, 35, 38, 40, 45
Gossett, Louis, Jr., 160, 161
Grant, Cary, 102, 108, 109, 109c, 202
Graves, Rupert, 170, 172
Grease, 267
Gregson-Williams, Harry, 234
Grusin, Dave, 156
Guinnes, Alec, 130

H

Hackford, Taylor, 160
Hackman, Gene, 140, 141
Hale, Alan, 24
Hamlisch, Marvin, 150
Hanks, Colin, 258
Hanks, Tom, 11, 109, 202, 203c, 204, 205c, 240
Hardwicke, Catherine, 270, 272
Harrison, Jim, 210
Harrison, Rex, 124, 126, 127, 129c
Hauer, Rutger, 174, 175, 175c, 176c, 177
Head, Edith, 91
Heckart, Eileen, 106
Hefti, Neal, 136
Henreid, Paul, 50
Hepburn, Audrey, 80, 80c, 82, 83c, 85, 86, 86c, 88, 89c, 91, 91c, 93c, 124, 125c, 126c, 127, 128, 129c
Hepburn, Katharine, 66, 66c, 68, 69, 69c, 71c, 102, 156, 157, 157c

Heymann, Werner, R., 48
Heywood, Pat, 142
High Society, 100, 102
Hiller, Arthur, 146, 148
Hoffman, Al, 56
Holden, William, 86, 88, 89c, 91c, 98, 99, 99c
Hollander, Frederick, 86
Holloway, Stanley, 124
Holm, Celeste, 100, 102
Holmes, Sherlock, 35
Hopkins, Anthony, 206, 208c
Horner, James, 206, 210, 222, 280
How the West Was Won, 73
Howards End, 170
Howard, James, Newton, 258
Howard, Leslie, 38, 40
Hunt, Linda, 212, 213
Hussey, Olivia, 142, 143c
Huston, Angelica, 69
Huston, John, 66
Hyde-White, Wilfrid, 124, 126c
Hyman, Dick, 178

I

IFC Films, 243
It Happened One Night, 12, 14, 22, 24, 27
It's A Wonderful Life, 27
It's Complicated, 244
I've Grown Accustomed to Her face, 128
Ivory, James, 170

J

Jackson, Peter, 258, 262
Jackson, Wilfred, 56, 94
Jarre, Maurice, 130, 131, 184
Jazz in Newport, 102
Jenson, Vicky, 234
Jeremiah Johnson, 164
Jerome, M.K., 50
Jeunet, Jean-Pierre, 252, 255
Jewison, Norman, 178
Jim Dear, 97
Joe Versus the Volcano, 204
Jones, Jennifer, 98, 99c
Jones, Tommy, Lee, 148

K

Kane, Carol, 152, 154
Karns, Roscoe, 24
Kazan, Lainie, 15, 240, 241
Keaton, Diane, 152, 153, 153c, 154, 155c, 244, 245c, 246, 246c, 248c
Keith, David, 160
Kelly, Grace, 100, 100c, 102, 102c, 105c
Kerr, Deborah, 108, 109, 109c
Key Largo, 69
King, Henry, 98
King Kong, 258, 260, 262
Kinski, Klaus, 130
Kirby, Bruno, 180
Kirkland, Sally, 151
Kretschmann, Thomas, 258
Kuhn, Judy, 212

L

Lady and The Tramp, 14, 94, 95, 97, 114
Ladyhawke, 174, 175, 177
Lagrange, Valérie, 134
Lai, Francis, 134, 146, 148
Lansbury, Angela, 194, 196
Lara's Theme, 131
Larkin, Linda, 198
Larson, Eric, 110
Lawrence of Arabia, 130, 218
Lean, David, 130
Lee, Peggy, 97
Legends of the Fall, 13, 14, 206, 210
Leigh, Vivien, 38, 38c, 40, 40c, 42c, 44, 44c, 45, 47c
Lelouch, Claude, 11, 134, 135
Lemmon, Jack, 138
Lerner, Alan, Jay, 124, 128
Lethal Weapon, 177

Lindfors, Viveca, 151
Lithgow, John, 234
Little Tramp, 18, 21, 22
Livingston, Jerry, 56
Lloyd, Phyllida, 264
Loewe, Frederick, 124, 128
Logan, Joshua, 106
Loggia, Robert, 160
Lopez, Trini, 204
Lord of the Rings, 250, 262
Loren, Sophia, 11, 13, 118, 119c, 120, 121, 121c, 122, 123c
Love Affair, 108
Love is a Many-Splendored Thing, 98, 99
Love Story, 146, 147, 148
Lubitsch, Ernst, 48
Lugosi, Bela, 48
Lund, John, 100
Luske, Hamilton, 56, 94

M
MacGraw, Ali, 146, 147, 147c, 148, 148c
Madden, John, 228
Mahoney, John, 178
Malinger, Ross, 202, 205c
Maltese Falcon, The, 69
Mamma Mia!, 264, 267
Man and a Woman, A, 134, 134
Manhattan Murder Mystery, 154
March, Fredric, 30, 32, 35
Marley, John, 146
Marshall, Garry, 188, 193
Mary Poppins, 128
Mastroianni, Marcello, 118, 119c, 121, 121c, 122, 123c
McCarey, Leo, 108
McDaniel, Hattie, 38, 40, 40c, 45
McDormand, Frances, 244, 245
McEnery, John, 142
McKeon, Doug, 156
McKern, Leo, 174
McLaglen, Victor, 72, 73, 75c
Means, Russell, 212
Menken, Alan, 194, 198, 212
Merchant, Ismail, 172
Merchant Ivory Productions, 170
Metro-Goldwyn-Mayer (MGM), 24, 30, 44, 48, 102, 130, 179
Meyer, Stephenie, 272
Myers, Nancy, 244
Milland, Ray, 146, 147
Minghella, Anthony, 218, 219
Miracle Worker, The, 141
Miramax Films, 220, 232
Mockridge, Cyril, J., 106
Monroe, Marilyn, 15, 91, 106, 107, 107c
Moonstruck, 178, 179
Moore, Demi, 184, 184c, 186, 187c
Mr. Smith Goes to Washington, 27
Murray, Don, 106, 107, 107c
Murphy, Eddie, 234, 236, 237c
Musker, John, 198
My Big Fat Greek Wedding, 15, 240, 241, 243
Myers, Harry, 18
Myers, Mike, 234, 237
My Fair Lady, 12, 124, 127, 128

N
Natwick, Mildred, 136
Nesbitt, Cathleen, 108
Newman, Alfred, 98, 106
Newport Jazz Festival, 102, 105
Nicholson, Jack, 244, 245, 245c, 246, 246c, 248c
Niehaus, Lennie, 216
Nineteenth Century Russia, 36c
Ninotchka, 38, 48
Nitzsche, Jack, 160
Nivola, Alessandro, 274, 275c, 276c
Nixon, Marni, 128
Norman, Marc, 232

O
O'Connell, Arthur, 106
Odd Couple, The, 138
O'Donnell, Rosie, 202, 204
Officer and a Gentleman, An, 160, 161
O'Hara, Maureen, 72, 73, 73c, 75c, 78, 79
O'Hara, Paige, 194
Oliver's Story, 147
Olivier, Laurence, 145
Ondaatje, Michael, 219
O'Neal, Marvin, 150
O'Neal, Patrick, 151
O'Neal, Ryan, 146, 147, 147c, 148, 148c
Orbach, Jerry, 194, 196
Ormond, Julia, 13, 206, 208, 210, 210c
O'Shea, Milo, 142
O'Sullivan, Maureen, 30, 35
Out of Africa, 13, 162, 164, 168

P
Paltrow, Gwyneth, 228, 229c, 231c, 232, 232c
Paramount Pictures, 80, 91, 138, 145, 148, 161, 186, 227
Parsons, Estelle, 140
Pasternak, Boris, 14, 130
Patterson, Neva, 108
Pattinson, Robert, 11, 270, 270c, 272c
Peck, Gregory, 80, 80c, 82, 83c, 85c
Peet, Amanda, 244, 246, 246c
Penn, Arthur, 140, 141
Peter Pan, 114
Pfeiffer, Michelle, 174, 175, 175c, 177c
Philadelphia, 204
Philadelphia Story, The, 102
Pica, Tina, 118
Pierce, David, Hyde, 204
Pitt, Brad, 14, 206, 206c, 208, 208c, 210c
Pixar Animation, 236
Pocahontas, 212, 214
Pocahontas II: Journey to a New World, 214
Poelvoorde, Benoît, 274, 275, 277
Pollack, S0ydney, 11, 150, 162, 164
Pollard, Michael, J., 140
Porter, Cole, 100
Powell, Andrew, 174
Powell, John, 234
Power, Hartley, 80
Prawer Jhabvala, Ruth, 172
Pretty Woman, 13, 188
Prince Rainer of Monaco, 102
Pullman, Bill, 202, 204
Pygmalion, 128

Q
Quiet Man, The, 72, 79
Quinn, Aidan, 206, 208, 208c, 210c

R
Raging Bull, 178
Rains, Claude, 50
Rathbone, Basil, 30, 35
Rawlings, Margaret, 80
Reaser, Elizabeth, 270
Redford, Robert, 136, 136c, 138, 139c, 150, 150c, 162, 163c, 164, 166c, 168, 169c
Reeves, Keanu, 244, 246c
Reiner, Rob, 180, 183, 204
Reitherman, Wolfgang, 110
Remains of the Day, The, 170
Republic Pictures, 79
Ribisi, Giovanni, 280
Rice, Tim, 198
Richardson, Ralph, 130
Rio Grande, 73
Roberts, Julia, 11, 13, 188, 189c, 191c, 193, 193c
Roberts, Tony, 152, 154
Robbins, Richard, 170
Robson, May, 30
Rodríguez, Michelle, 280
Roman Holiday, 13, 22, 80

R (cont.)
Romeo and Juliet, 12, 142, 145, 228, 230
Room with a View, A, 13, 170, 172
Rosemary's Baby, 148
Rosenberg, Melissa, 272
Rota, Nino, 142
Rush, Geoffrey, 228, 232
Ryan, Meg, 10, 11, 109, 180, 180c, 181, 183, 183c, 202, 203c, 205c
Ryddel, Mark, 156

S
Sabrina, 13, 86, 88, 91
Saks, Gene, 136
Saldaña, Zoë, 280, 281, 282c
Salvietti, Agostino, 118
San Giacomo, Laura, 188
Sandler, Adam, 250, 251, 251c
Sands, Julian, 170, 171c, 172
Saturday Night Fever, 178
Saving Private Ryan, 232
Schneider, Rob, 250
Scholl, Jack, 50
Scott Thomas, Kristin, 218, 219, 219c, 221c
Segal, Erich, 147, 148
Segal, Peter, 250
Seinfeld, 193
Selznick, David, O., 35
Seven Year Itch, The, 91
Seyfried, Amanda, 264, 268c
Shaiman, Marc, 180, 202
Shakespeare in Love, 210, 220, 228, 232
Shakespeare, William, 140, 142, 144c, 228, 231c
Shanley, John, Patrick, 179
Sharif, Omar, 11, 14, 130, 131, 132c
Shaw, Bernard, George, 128
Shoeshine, 122
Shrek, 234, 236
Silverman, Sid, 14
Silvers, Louis, 24
Simon, Neil, 138
Simon, Paul, 152, 154
Sinatra, Frank, 100, 102, 105c
Sire, Antoine, 134
Skarsgård, Stellan, 264
Sleeper, 152
Sleeping Beauty, 110, 114
Sleepless in Seattle, 109, 202, 204
Smith, John, 212
Smith, Maggie, 170, 172
Smith, Paul, J., 56
Something's Gotta Give, 244
Somewhere My Love, 131
Sony Pictures, 204, 277
Sony Pictures' Tristar, 206
SOS, 264
Sound of Music, The, 130
Stagecoach, 38, 73
Stalag 17, 99
Steiger, Rod, 130
Steiner, Max, 38, 50
Stewart, Jimmy, 27
Stewart, Kristen, 11, 270, 270c, 272c
Stiers, David, Ogden, 196, 212
Sting, The, 138
Stoppard, Tom, 232
Stothart, Herbert, 30
Streep, Meryl, 11, 13, 162, 163c, 164, 165c, 166c, 168, 169c, 216, 217, 217c, 264, 265c, 266c, 267, 268c
Streisand, Barbra, 150, 150c, 151
Strouse, Charles, 140
Summit Entertainment, 272
Superman, 177
Suyin, Han, 99
Swayze, Patrick, 184, 184c, 186, 187c

T
20th Century Fox, 22, 99, 106, 108, 175, 220, 227, 281
Tautou, Audrey, 11, 13, 252, 252c, 255, 256, 256c, 274, 275, 275c, 276c, 277, 279c

Thatcher, Torin, 98
Thomas, Henry, 206, 208c
Thompson, Francis, 99
Titanic, 12, 142, 210, 222, 225, 227, 281
Tolstoy, Leo, 30
Tootoosis, Gordon, 206
Travolta, John, 267
Treasure of Sierra Madre, The, 69
Trintignant, Jean-Louis, 134, 135, 135c
Trousdale, Gary, 194
Trovajoli, Armando, 118
Twilight, 11, 270, 272

U
Ulliel, Gaspard, 252, 254c
Ulvaeus, Bjorn, 264
Universal Pictures, 156, 164, 232, 262, 264
Universal/Miramax, 228
United Artists, 69

V
Vardalos, Nia, 15, 240, 241, 241c, 243, 243c
Variety, 14
Veidt, Conrad, 50
Very Long Engagement, A, 13, 252, 255, 256

W
Walken, Christopher, 152, 154
Wallace, Oliver, 56, 94
Walt Disney, 64, 94, 110, 193, 198, 212, 215c, 220, 236
Walters, Charles, 100
Walters, Julie, 264
Warbeck, Stephen, 228
Warner Bros., 50, 128, 141, 175, 216, 277
Warren, Harry, 108
Waterloo, 264
Watts, Naomi, 258, 258c, 260, 262c
Way We Were, The, 150, 151
Wayne, John, 72, 73, 73c, 75c, 78, 79
Weaver, Sigourney, 152, 154, 280
Wedding Singer, The, 251
Weinger, Scott, 198
Welker, Frank, 198
What Women Want, 244
When Harry Met Sally..., 10, 11, 180, 183, 204
White, Richard, 194
Whiting, Leonard, 142, 143c
Wilder, Billy, 11, 80, 91
Wilder, Gene, 140, 141
Williams, Harcourt, 80
Williams, John, 86
Williams, Robin, 198
Wilkinson, Tom, 228
Wilson, Dooley, 52
Wilson, Rita, 204, 240
Winger, Debra, 160, 161, 161c
Winslet, Kate, 142, 222, 223c, 225, 225c, 226c
Wise, Kirk, 194
With a Little Bit of Luck, 128
Wizard of Oz, The, 38
Wood, John, 174, 175
Woods, James, 151
Worthington, Sam, 280, 280c, 281, 282c
Wuthering Heights, 38

Y
Yared, Gabriel, 218
Yesterday, Today and Tomorrow, 13, 118, 119c, 121, 122
York, Michael, 142, 145
Young, Victor, 72, 80

Z
Zaentz, Saul, 220
Zane, Billy, 222
Zeffirelli, Franco, 11, 12, 142, 145
Zimmer, Hans, 244
Zucker, Jerry, 184
Zwick, Edward, 206, 210
Zwick, Joel, 240

Pictures/Album/Contrasto * **Page 163** Archives du 7eme Art/Photos12.com * **Page 164** Collection Cinema/Photos12.com * **Page 165** MCA/Universal/Everett Collection/Contrasto * **Page 166** Collection CSFF/Rue des Archives * **Page 167** Archives du 7eme Art/Photos12.com * **Page 168** IFPA/Agefotostock/Marka * **Page 169** Archives du 7eme Art/Photos12.com * **Page 171** Cinecom/courtesy Everett Collection/Contrasto * **Page 172** Cinecom/courtesy Everett Collection/Contrasto * **Pages 172-173** Merchant Ivory/Goldcrest/Album/Contrasto * **Page 175** Warner Bros. Pictures/courtesy Everett Collection/Contrasto * **Page 176** Warner Bros. Pictures/courtesy Everett Collection/Contrasto * **Page 177** 20th Century Fox/Album/Contrasto * **Page 179 top** MGM/courtesy Everett Collection/Contrasto * **Page 179 bottom** MGM/courtesy Everett Collection/Contrasto * **Page 181** Archives du 7eme Art/Photos12.com * **Page 182** IFPA/Agefotostock/Marka * **Page 183** Collection Cinéma/Photos12.com * **Page 185** RDA/Rue des Archives * **Page 186** Collection Cinéma/Photos12.com * **Page 187** Everett Collection/Contrasto * **Page 189** Sipa Press/LaPresse * **Page 190** Touchstone/Warners/Album/Contrasto * **Page 191** Buena Vista Pictures/Courtesy Everett Collection/Contrasto * **Page 192** Buena Vista Pictures/Courtesy Everett Collection/Contrasto * **Page 193** Sipa Press/LaPresse * **Page 195** Collection Cinéma/Photos12.com * **Page 196** Buena Vista Pictures/Courtesy Everett Collection/Contrasto * **Page 197** Buena Vista Pictures/Courtesy Everett Collection/Contrasto * **Page 199** Walt Disney Productions/Album/Contrasto * **Pages 200-201** Archives du 7eme Art/Photos12.com * **Page 203** TriStar Pictures/Album/Contrasto * **Page 205 top** Collection Cinéma/Photos12.com * **Page 205 bottom** TriStar/courtesy Everett Collection/Contrasto * **Page 207** Corbis Sygma/Corbis * **Page 208** TriStar/courtesy Everett Collection/Contrasto * **Page 209** TriStar Pictures/Album/Contrasto * **Page 210** Dimension Films/Courtesy Everett Collection/Contrasto * **Page 211** TriStar/courtesy Everett Collection/Contrasto * **Page 213** Everett Collection/Contrasto * **Page 214** Walt Disney Productions/Album/Contrasto * **Pages 214-215** Walt Disney Productions/Album/Contrasto * **Page 217** RDA/Rue des Archives * **Page 219** Miramax/Album/Contrasto * **Page 220** Miramax/Courtesy Everett Collection/Contrasto * **Page 221** Miramax/Courtesy Everett Collection/Contrasto * **Page 223** Paramount/20th Century Fox/Album/Contrasto * **Pages 224-225** Archives du 7eme Art/Photos12.com * **Page 225** Starstock/Photoshot * **Pages 226-227** Paramount/20th Century Fox/Album/Contrasto * **Page 229** Archives du 7eme Art/Photos12.com * **Page 230** Miramax/Courtesy Everett Collection/Contrasto * **Page 231** Miramax/Courtesy Everett Collection/Contrasto * **Page 233 top** Miramax/Courtesy Everett Collection/Contrasto * **Page 233 bottom** Archives du 7eme Art/Photos12.com * **Page 235** Splash/Olycom * **Page 236** DreamWorks/Courtesy Everett Collection/Contrasto * **Page 237** DreamWorks/Courtesy Everett Collection/Contrasto * **Pages 238-239** DreamWorks/Courtesy Everett Collection/Contrasto * **Page 241** IFC Films/Album/Contrasto * **Pages 242-243** IFC Films/Album/Contrasto * **Page 243** Everett Collection/Contrasto * **Page 245** IFPA/Agefotostock/Marka * **Page 246** Columbia Pictures/Courtesy Everett Collection/Contrasto * **Page 247** Columbia Pictures/Courtesy Everett Collection/Contrasto * **Page 248** IFPA/Agefotostock/Marka * **Pages 248-249** Columbia Pictures/Courtesy Everett Collection/Contrasto * **Page 251** Darren Michaels/Columbia Pictures/Album/Contrasto * **Page 253** Bruno Calvo/Warner Bros./Album/Contrasto * **Pages 254-255** Bruno Calvo/Warner Bros./Album/Contrasto * **Page 255** Warner Independent Pictures/courtesy Everett Collection/Contrasto * **Page 257** Bruno Calvo/Warner Bros./Album/Contrasto * **Pages 259** Archives du 7eme Art/Photos12.com * **Page 260** Foto Blitz/Agefotostock/Marka * **Page 261** Foto Blitz/Agefotostock/Marka * **Page 262** Archives du 7eme Art/Photos12.com * **Pages 262-263** Archives du 7eme Art/Photos12.com * **Page 265** Littlestar Productions/Playtone/Album/Contrasto * **Page 266** Universal/courtesy Everett Collection/Contrasto * **Page 267** IFPA/Agefotostock/Marka * **Page 268** Littlestar Productions/Playtone/Album/Contrasto * **Page 269** IFPA/Agefotostock/Marka * **Page 271** Imprint Entertainment/Maverick Films/Summit Entertainment/Album/Contrasto * **Page 272** Archives du 7eme Art/Photos12.com * **Page 273** Archives du 7eme Art/Photos12.com * **Page 275** Archives du 7eme Art/Photos12.com * **Page 276** Unimedia International/Olycom * **Page 277** Archives du 7eme Art/Photos12.com * **Pages 278-279** Archives du 7eme Art/Photos12.com * **Page 281** 20th Century Fox/Courtesy Everett Collection/Contrasto * **Pages 282-283** Rex Features/Olycom * **Cover** © Archives du 7eme Art/Photos12.com

ROBERT MARICH

FILM JOURNALIST/ANALYST ROBERT MARICH HAS A QUARTER CENTURY EXPERIENCE WRITING ABOUT FILM AND MEDIA FROM THE UNITED STATES, EUROPE AND ASIA.
HE IS AUTHOR OF MARKETING TO MOVIEGOERS, WHICH IS A BUSINESS BOOK ABOUT THEATRICAL RELEASING THAT IS IN ITS SECOND EDITION, AND ITS ASSOCIATED PROFESSIONAL INFORMATION WEBSITE WWW.MARKETINGMOVIES.NET. HE ALSO SERVED AS LEAD EDITOR UPDATING A COLLEGE TEXTBOOK ABOUT CAREERS IN THE MUSIC BUSINESS. MARICH'S MOVIE INDUSTRY ARTICLES HAVE BEEN PUBLISHED IN THE LOS ANGELES TIMES NEWSPAPER, VARIETY, HOLLYWOOD REPORTER AND LONDON-BASED SCREEN INTERNATIONAL. DURING HIS CAREER, MARICH HAS COVERED LEADING FILM FESTIVALS AND FILM/TV PROGRAM MARKETS AROUND THE WORLD AS AN ACCREDITED JOURNALIST. HE IS A GUEST LECTURER AT COLLEGES ON MEDIA TOPICS.
NOW BASED IN THE NEW YORK CITY AREA, MARICH HAS COVERED FILM WHILE LIVING IN LOS ANGELES, LONDON AND NEW YORK. HE IS A MEMBER OF THE AUTHORS GUILD, WHICH IS THE CENTURY-OLD ORGANIZATION FOR BOOK WRITERS IN THE UNITED STATES.

The author would like to acknowledge two people for their invaluable assistance. My wife Marie Silverman Marich—who worked as a professional copywriter and journalist at Variety—provided valuable proofing of text. Also, my thanks goes to Laura Accomazzo at White Star Publishers for guiding me and this book.